Starting Statistics

Starting Statistics

A Short, Clear Guide

Neil Burdess

Los Angeles | London | New Delhi
Singapore | Washington DC

SAGE Publications Ltd
1 Oliver's Yard
55 City Road
London EC1Y 1SP

SAGE Publications Inc.
2455 Teller Road
Thousand Oaks, California 91320

SAGE Publications India Pvt Ltd
B 1/I 1 Mohan Cooperative Industrial Area
Mathura Road
New Delhi 110 044

SAGE Publications Asia-Pacific Pte Ltd
33 Pekin Street #02-01
Far East Square
Singapore 048763

Library of Congress Control Number Available

British Library Cataloguing in Publication data

A catalogue record for this book is available from the British Library

ISBN 978-1-84920-097-4
ISBN 978-1-84920-098-1(pbk)

Typeset by C&M Digitals (P) Ltd, Chennai, India
Printed in Great Britain by CPI Antony Rowe, Chippenham, Wiltshire
Printed on paper from sustainable resources

To the memory of Jessie, Doug and Norman

Contents

Welcome to *Starting Statistics*

Statistics are everywhere as we delight in measuring anything and everything. For example, I learned this morning that 40% of 3-month old babies in the USA regularly watch television, and that on average Chinese people have their first kiss at 23 years of age. The trend to measure and quantify has also happened in colleges and universities, where an increasing number of students in arts, business, education, and health are directed (rather than choose) to become familiar with some of the basic tools of statistical analysis.

Unfortunately, becoming familiar with some of the basic tools of statistical analysis for many students is on the same level as stroking spiders, and a bit lower than going to the dentist or speaking in public! You will often see terms such as *numerophobia, math(s) anxiety,* and *sadistics* bandied around. This is a pity because many of the concepts that underlie statistical analysis are not particularly complex. The aim of this little book is to show that the basics of statistics are something that virtually everyone can handle with a bit of time and effort.

In the previous paragraph, I used the word *little* in a positive sense. Indeed, the 'most widely read statistics book in the history of the world' is Darrell Huff's classic text *How To Lie With Statistics,* which Michael Steele describes as a 'slim volume' (2005: 205). Slimness is also important in *Starting Statistics* as the book's aim is to explain as clearly and briefly as possible the basic ideas behind the statistics.

Starting Statistics shows that statistics are not the product of some black magic but, instead, are the result of some very basic arithmetic. None of the calculations in the book include *xs* or *ys*, because you don't need them to understand what's going on. Actually doing the calculations is just hack-work – and computers can do that much more quickly and accurately than you or I can. It's the intellectual questions that come before and after the calculations that are important. The most basic questions are:

- What are the best statistics to use with my data?
- What do the calculated statistics tell me?

Basically, statistics help people see the wood rather than the trees, the group rather than the individual. For example, imagine trying to describe what you see below to a friend on the telephone:

If all you see are meaningless, irregular grey shapes, your description will be long and complicated. However, if you see the word LIFE in white on a grey background, then your description will be short and simple. Similarly, when looking at a mass of numbers, your aim is to make sense of them by identifying the overall pattern using statistics.

I see two types of readers using *Starting Statistics*. You may be a student enrolled on a stats course for which this book is a set text. In this case, your instructors will guide you through the chapters. Alternatively, you may be about to start a stats course, and are stressed just thinking about it! You want a book that will give you some clear and sensible advice about statistics. If so, you've found what you're looking for. I suggest that you read *Starting Statistics* from cover to cover over a period of a week or two. Start slowly, building up speed as you become more comfortable with the ideas. There are no exercises, no calculations, no discussion questions, no self-tests. If you focus on the job in hand, you will be able to understand the vast majority of the book on first reading. At the end of the week or fortnight, you will be in an excellent position to embark on your course with *confidence*, an important element in any study – and particularly with statistics!

Starting Statistics has a very straightforward structure. There are five basic parts:

Part I   *Measurement* This part focuses on answering two basic questions about a set of data: (i) What's the most typical value? (ii) How typical is it?

Part II   *Standardisation* This part focuses on the widespread practice of changing how things are measured to make the results easier to understand.

Part III   *Correlations* This part focuses on describing the relationship between two characteristics using graphs and numbers. In other words, how much better can you predict one set of values once you know a second set of values?

Part IV   *Sampling and estimation* This part focuses on how to draw a sample from a population, and then how to estimate characteristics about this population from the sample.

Part V   *Hypothesis testing* This part focuses on how to draw up a hypothesis, or testable prediction about a population, and then work out the likelihood that it is correct using the results from a sample.

Within each part, the main organising device is the very simple but very important distinction between information in the form of named categories and information in the form of numbers. For example, information about your country of birth is in named categories (e.g. USA, UK, Australia) and information about how many millions of people live there is in numbers (e.g. 300, 60, 20). After a short introductory chapter, each part usually divides into a chapter about categories and a chapter about numbers.

To make sure that I follow my own advice to keep the book 'slim', I'll stop now, and let you get going on *Starting Statistics*.

Neil Burdess

Part One

Measurement

ONE

Introducing measurement

Chapter Overview

This chapter will:

- Introduce some useful Jargon – units of analysis, variables, values.
- Describe different levels of measurement – nominal, ordinal, interval.
- Show how to identify the overall pattern in a set of data by asking: (i) What's the most typical value? (ii) How do the rest of the values spread out around it?

Social researchers study three broad areas: (i) what people *think* (e.g. their attitudes, values, prejudices), (ii) what people *do* (e.g. their behaviour as voters, consumers, workers), and (iii) what people *are* (e.g. their age, social class, health status). Social researchers collect information in two basic ways: (i) they ask people questions; and (ii) they observe people, either directly or indirectly through the things they've made.

For example, imagine that you are interested in researching movies. Thus, movies are the *units of analysis*. If you go to the comprehensive Internet Movie Database, you can find answers to a range of questions about each movie. For example:

- Where was the main film studio located?
- What was the classification rating for public exhibition?
- What was the length (or *running time*) of the movie?

As Table 1.1 shows, there is a variety of answers to each question. For example, the main film studio for *Harry Potter* was in the UK, while that for the *Lion King* was in the USA. A characteristic that varies (e.g. studio location) is a *variable*. The numbers or words used to measure the variable are *values* (e.g. UK, US). Together, values are referred to as *data*. These bits of jargon are useful to remember.

Table 1.1 shows information about three characteristics for 5 of the 100 most commercially successful movies. Using the jargon, Table 1.1 shows data about three variables for five units of analysis. Notice that numbers alone occur in just one column. Variables described by numbers are *numerical* variables (or *quantitative*

Table 1.1 Units of analysis, variables and values

| Units of analysis – movies | Variables – characteristics that vary | | |
	Studio location	Exhibition rating[1]	Running time (min)
Harry Potter and the Sorcerer's Stone	UK	Parental guidance (PG)	152
Lion King	USA	General (G)	89
Lord of the Rings: The Return of the King	NZ	Parents strongly cautioned (PG-13)	201
Pirates of the Caribbean: Dead Man's Chest	USA	Parents strongly cautioned (PG-13)	150
Dark Knight	USA	Parents strongly cautioned (PG-13)	152

[1]Exhibition ratings for USA. 'General' is classified 'Universal' in UK. 'Parents strongly cautioned' is classified 'Under-12s need accompanying adult (12A)' in UK, and 'Mature' in Australia.

Source: IMDb 2009a

variables). The other columns contain category names instead of numbers. Variables described by category names are *categorical* variables (or *qualitative* variables). The next section looks in more detail at the various *levels* at which you can measure variables.

Levels of measurement

One of the simplest ways to analyse the information about the movies' *Studio location* is to label boxes with the name of each country listed in the 100 database records. You write out each film's studio location on a separate card, and place the card into the appropriate box (e.g. all the US cards go into the box marked 'USA'). When you have distributed all 100 cards, it's easy to count the number of cards in each box, and see how many films were made in the USA, how many in the UK, and so on. You can then order the boxes from the one with the largest number of cards to the one with the smallest number.

Notice, however, that you can put the countries into order only *after* you've finished counting the cards. Before counting, you can put the boxes showing the countries in any order (e.g. USA, UK, NZ...; or UK, NZ, USA...). All you can say about the different countries is that they are different. There is no reason why you should always list them in a particular order. When categories are unordered like this, and the only thing you can say is that they have different names, the data are at the *nominal level of measurement* (from the Latin word *nominalis*, meaning 'to do with names').

The *Exhibition rating* variable on Table 1.1 is a bit different. You label one box 'General', another 'Parental guidance' the third 'Parents strongly cautioned', and so on if there are other exhibition ratings on the list of movies. Once again, imagine that you put the rating for each of the 100 movies on a card, and then put each card into the appropriate box. You then count the number of cards in each box.

However, the difference between exhibition rating and studio location is that you can put the rating boxes in order *before* you distribute the cards. The ratings are categorised in terms of how explicitly the films depict violence, sex, and so on. Thus, a movie rated 'Parents strongly cautioned' is more explicit than one rated 'Parental guidance' (PG), and a PG-rated film is more explicit than one rated 'General' (G). So, not only are the categories different, but they also have a built-in order – an order that is apparent *before* you begin the counting process. When you can order the categories in this way, the data are at the *ordinal level of measurement*. Notice, however, that although you can say that a PG-rated film is more explicit than a G-rated film, you can't say *how much more* explicit.

BEHIND THE STATS

One bizarre story that centres on ordinal level of measurement originated in 2006 when the International Astronomical Union (IAU) downgraded Pluto from a *full planet* to a *dwarf planet*. This led to a remarkable outcry, including a petition calling on the IAU to reverse the decision (PleaseSavePluto 2008). It generated a new word, to be *plutoed*, meaning to be demoted or devalued, which was the American Dialect Society's 'Word of the year' in 2006 (ADS 2007). In 2008, the IAU in part bowed to this pressure, and introduced a new class of planets, *plutoids*, lying between full planets and dwarf planets, the founding member of which is – Pluto (IAU 2008). Smaller than dwarf planets are the *minor planets*, of which 15,000 have been named. There are many mnemonics (memory aids) for the order of the planets from the Sun. The one I use is: My Very Easy Memory Jogger Still Uses Nine Planets (Mercury, Venus, Earth, Mars, Jupiter, Saturn, Uranus, Neptune, Pluto).

Table 1.1 also shows each movie's *Running time* in minutes. You can follow the same procedure as before, labelling boxes (e.g. '152', '89') and placing each film into the appropriate box. However, these running time values are very different from the studio location and exhibition rating categories. The difference between any pair of numbers not only shows that one movie is shorter or longer than the other, but also shows *how much* shorter or longer. For example, you know that a 152 minute movie is 63 minutes longer than an 89 minute movie. When you can measure the difference (or 'interval') between any two values, the data are at the *interval level of measurement*.

Table 1.2 summarises the type of information given by variables at the nominal, ordinal, and interval levels of measurement. Clearly, interval data contain more information than ordinal data, and much more than nominal data.

Social researchers are most likely to work with nominal data. For example, a recent Census form contained approximately 50 questions, three-quarters of which asked for nominal-level answers. Table 1.3 shows some of them. The level of measurement is very important because what types of analysis researchers can

Table 1.2   Information at different levels of measurement

Information about	Level of measurement		
	Nominal	Ordinal	Interval
Difference (i.e. same or different?)	✓	✓	✓
Direction of difference (i.e. more or less?)		✓	✓
Degree of difference (i.e. how much more or less?)			✓

do is very dependent on what sort of data they have. This is why there are separate chapters in this book for numerical (i.e. interval) variables and categorical (i.e. nominal and ordinal) variables.

Table 1.3   Levels of measurement – Census questions

(a) Nominal data

1 Are you male or female?
2 What is your relationship to the household head? (e.g. Spouse, De facto partner, Boarder)
3 What is your marital status? (e.g. Never married, Married, Widowed)
4 In which country were you born? (e.g. Australia, England, New Zealand)
5 What is your religion? (e.g. Catholic, Anglican, Uniting)
6 What is the main field of study for your highest qualification completed? (e.g. Plumbing, History, Hairdressing)
7 Which best describes the industry or business of the employer at the location where you work? (e.g. Manufacturing, Retailing, Health)
8 How did you get to work last Tuesday? (e.g. Train, Bus, Car)
9 In the last two weeks, did you spend time looking after a child, without pay? (No; Yes, looked after my own child; Yes, looked after a child other than my own)
10 In the last 12 months, did you spend any time doing voluntary work through an organisation or group? (No, Yes)

(b) Ordinal data

1 How well do you speak English? (Very well, Well, Not well, Not at all)
2 Do you ever need someone to help with, or be with you for, self-care everyday activities such as eating, showering, dressing or toileting? (Yes always, Yes sometimes, No)
3 What is the level of the highest qualification you have completed? (e.g. Trade certificate, Advanced diploma, Degree)

(c) Interval data

1 What was your age last birthday?
2 What is the total income you usually receive per week?

Source: Based on ABS 2006

Distributions

Spend a minute or so trying to work out what Figure 1.1 shows. Then imagine trying to describe the figure to a friend over the telephone.

If all you see is a meaningless mass of irregular grey shapes, your telephone description will be long and complicated. However, if you see the word LIFE in

Figure 1.1   Identifying an overall pattern

white on a grey background, then your description will be short and simple. Similarly, when looking at a mass of numbers or category names, your aim is to make sense of them by identifying the overall pattern. The term for this overall pattern is *distribution*, because you are describing how the values are distributed across the range of categories or numbers.

Table 1.4(a) shows the populations of the 50 states in the USA. The states are in alphabetical order, from Alabama (population 4.7 million) to Wyoming (0.5 million). Numerically, this means that the values are in random order. As it stands,

Table 1.4   US states, estimated population

1.4(a) Data in random order

AL[1]	4.7[2]	HI	1.3	MA	6.5	NM	2.0	SD	0.8
AK	0.7	ID	1.5	MI	10.0	NY	19.5	TN	6.2
AZ	6.5	IL	12.9	MN	5.2	NC	9.2	TX	24.3
AR	2.9	IN	6.4	MS	2.9	ND	0.6	UT	2.7
CA	36.9	IA	3.0	MO	5.9	OH	11.5	VT	0.6
CO	4.9	KS	2.8	MT	1.0	OK	3.6	VA	7.8
CT	3.5	KY	4.3	NE	1.8	OR	3.8	WA	6.5
DE	0.9	LA	4.4	NV	2.6	PA	12.4	WV	1.8
FL	18.3	ME	1.3	NH	1.3	RI	1.1	WI	5.6
GA	9.7	MD	5.6	NJ	8.7	SC	4.5	WY	0.5

1.4(b) Data in rank order

WY	0.5	ME	1.3	IA	3.0	WI	5.6	NC	9.2
VT	0.6	ID	1.5	CT	3.5	MD	5.6	GA	9.7
ND	0.6	NE	1.8	OK	3.6	MO	5.9	MI	10.0
AK	0.7	WV	1.8	OR	3.8	TN	6.2	OH	11.5
SD	0.8	NM	2.0	KY	4.3	IN	6.4	PA	12.4
DE	0.9	NV	2.6	LA	4.4	AZ	6.5	IL	12.9
MT	1.0	UT	2.7	SC	4.5	MA	6.5	FL	18.3
RI	1.1	KS	2.8	AL	4.7	WA	6.5	NY	19.5
HI	1.3	AR	2.9	CO	4.9	VA	7.8	TX	24.3
NH	1.3	MS	2.9	MN	5.2	NJ	8.7	CA	36.9

[1] States listed using official US Postal Service abbreviations (USPS 1998).
[2] Population estimates in millions.

Source: US Census Bureau 2008a

Table 1.4(a) is not very informative in terms of describing the overall distribution of the numbers. It's the equivalent of seeing Figure 1.1 as a mass of irregular grey shapes on a white background. If I asked you for an overall description of the 50 values, I suspect that you wouldn't be able to say a great deal. You need to organise the data so that you can more clearly see the distribution of the values.

BEHIND THE STATS

Alphabetical order is random in the sense that there is no inherent order in the positioning of letters in the alphabet. We place A first and Z last, but there is no reason why the letters *have* to be in this order. Moreover, what places are called can often be the result of chance events. For example, the name 'Idaho' was first proposed for what eventually became Colorado; and the name 'Montana' was first proposed for what eventually became Idaho. No one seems to know how the name Idaho originated (see Wells nd).

The simplest way to help you see the distribution more clearly is to place the values in *rank order*, starting with the smallest, then the second smallest, and so on, ending with the largest. A ranked list such as this is called an *array*. Table 1.4(b) shows an array of the US state population totals, starting with the smallest, Wyoming (0.5 million), and ending with the largest, California (36.9 million). The array helps you answer two basic questions about the distribution of values:

1   What is the most typical value?
2   How do the rest of the values spread out around the most typical value?

For example, you could say that the most typical value was the one in the exact centre of the array. The array in Table 1.4(b) has 50 values, and is centred midway between the 25th and 26th values. As the 25th value is *4.3* and the 26th is *4.4*, the array centres on a population of *4.35*. This most typical value is the *median*. The simplest way to measure how the rest of the values spread out around this central value is to find the difference between the largest population (36.9) and the smallest (0.5), a statistic known as the *overall range* (36.9 – 0.5 = 36.4). This indicates the large spread of US state populations, with the most typical being much nearer the minimum than the maximum size.

You need different methods when describing the distribution of numbers in a numerical variable and describing the distribution of categories in a categorical variable. The next two chapters look in detail at how to measure distributions in numerical and categorical variables.

TWO

Measuring numbers

| **Chapter Overview** |

This chapter will:

- Emphasise the importance of identifying the overall pattern in a set of numbers by asking: (i) What's the most typical value? (ii) How do the rest of the values spread out around it?
- Show how to find the most typical value using the *mean* and the *median*.
- Compare the relative strengths and weaknesses of the mean and median.
- Show how to measure the spread of data around the median using the *midspread*, and around the mean using the *standard deviation*.
- Compare the relative strengths and weaknesses of the midspread and standard deviation.

Chapter 1 pointed out that there are two basic ways of measuring variables. For example, a person's age is measured by numbers (e.g. 19). Age is thus a *numerical variable*. In contrast, a person's religion is 'measured' using named categories (e.g. Christian). Religion is thus a *categorical variable*. This chapter focuses on numerical variables, and the following chapter on categorical variables.

Table 2.1 shows the essay marks achieved by 52 university students. The marks are in the order they appear in the course co-ordinator's gradebook, which lists the students alphabetically by family name, from Tony Abbott (who has not done well, scoring only 32%) to Whitney Wilson (who has done better, scoring 67%).

Table 2.1   Marks shown on an alphabetical student list

32	74	63	51	51	96	69	52	42	70	56	84	41
53	65	65	39	46	63	51	55	58	75	50	75	76
46	34	64	71	66	47	28	71	55	56	56	67	66
56	34	86	38	72	61	65	56	58	59	49	45	67

Source: Hypothetical (i.e. I made them up!)

As they stand, the numbers in Table 2.1 are not very helpful in answering the following basic questions:

- What's the most typical value? In other words, what's the central or average mark – the single value that by itself best describes all the marks in the list?
- How do the rest of the values spread out around the most typical value? For example, how *far* do the rest of the values spread out above and below the most typical value? Are all the marks fairly similar and thus bunched together, or is there a wide spread of marks?

This chapter looks in detail at how to answer these basic questions when you are dealing with numerical variables.

What's the most typical value?

This section focuses on the question: 'What's the most typical value?' It outlines two ways to answer this question: the very familiar *mean*, and the slightly less familiar *median*.

Mean

The most familiar way to work out the most typical value, or average, is to calculate the *mean*. Indeed, in everyday speech the average *is* the mean. In effect, the mean is what you get when you share out everything equally among all the individuals in a group. As I'm sure you know, to work out the mean you go through three steps:

1 Add together all the values (the result is known as the *sum*).
2 Count the number of values (the *count*).
3 Divide the sum by the count (the *mean*).

So, to find the mean of the student marks in Table 2.1, add together all the marks (3025) and divide by the number of students (52):

$$\text{Mean} = \frac{\text{Sum}}{\text{Count}} = \frac{\text{Total marks}}{\text{Number of students}} = \frac{3025}{52} = 58.2$$

In fact, 3025 divided by 52 is 58.17307... . The above answer is *rounded off* to 58.2. The convention is to round off answers to one digit more than there are in the original values, as a more detailed result can give a misleading impression of accuracy. Because the marks are in tens and units (e.g. 28), the mean is in tens, units and tenths (58.2).

A common *rounding rule* is: '0 to 4 down; 5 to 9 up'. The '0 to 4' and '5 to 9' refer to the value immediately to the right of the one you are rounding to. For example, if you are rounding to the nearest tenth (i.e. the first digit after the decimal place) you have to take note of the hundredth value (i.e. the second digit after the decimal place). Round down 9.6̲0, 9.6̲1, 9.6̲2, 9.6̲3, and 9.6̲4 to 9.6

because the hundredth values are between 0 and 4. And round up 9.65, 9.66, 9.67, 9.68, and 9.69 to 9.7 because the hundredth values are between 5 and 9. The mean of the student marks includes seven-hundredths (58.17...). You thus round up to the next tenth – 58.17 is rounded up to 58.2. Chapter 6 says more about rounding.

Median

Occasionally the mean is not an ideal measure of the most typical value. Consider the following values:

39	40	42	43	44	46	48	49	49	600

What's the most typical value? The mean is 100 (1000 ÷ 10). But it's not a good summary of the set of numbers because it's more than twice as large as nine of the values and six times smaller than the tenth one. The problem, of course, is that the mean is greatly influenced by the one very large value (600).

In these circumstances, a better way to work out the most typical value is to use the *median*. You may have come across the word in terms of a median strip – land running down the middle of a road. Similarly, in statistics the median is the middle value when you rank a set of numbers from smallest to largest. For example, in the set of 10 values above, the two middle values are 44 (ranked fifth) and 46 (ranked sixth). The median is thus half-way between these: (44 + 46) ÷ 2 = 45.

Median

39	40	42	43	44	46	48	49	49	600

45

You often see medians used to describe house prices. This is because, compared to the mean, the median is less influenced by the very high prices of large houses in expensive suburbs. The downside to using the median is that the absolute values (e.g. 39, 40, 42) are largely forgotten. It's the relative values that are important (e.g. first, second, third). Thus, in the above example, it doesn't matter what the first four values or last four values are; the median will still be the same providing the middle two values remain the same. For example:

Median

9	10	12	13	44	46	598	599	599	600

45

Median

0.09	0.10	1.20	1.30	44	46	598,000	599,000	599,000	600,000

45

The significance of this is told by Stephen Jay Gould, a prominent American scientist, in his 'personal story of statistics' (Gould 1985). His doctors told him that he was suffering from an incurable cancer, 'with a median mortality of only eight months after discovery'. As you might imagine, his initial shocked reaction was 'I will probably be dead in eight months' (p. 40).

But then he thought more carefully about the phrase 'median mortality of only eight months after discovery'. What does it actually mean? He soon realised that it means that half the patients live less than eight months, and half live *more* than eight months. As he was young, had been diagnosed early, and had access to the best medical treatment, he knew that he had a good chance of living more than eight months. Most importantly, he realised that although half the deaths 'must be scrunched up between zero and eight months', the other half (above the median) 'can extend out for years and years' (p. 41). In fact, Stephen Jay Gould died 20 years later from a completely unrelated cause. It wasn't that his doctors had made a mistake with the earlier diagnosis. As Figure 2.1 shows, it was simply the way in which a median is worked out.

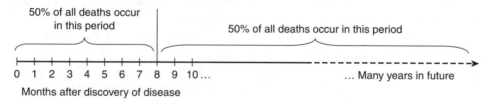

Figure 2.1 'Median mortality of only eight months'

Mean or median – which is better?

The two methods of identifying the most typical value both have strengths and weaknesses:

1 Mean – uses all the data, but is strongly influenced by extreme values.
2 Median – not influenced by extreme values, but uses relative rather than absolute values for all but the middle values.

Which is better, mean or median, depends on the values in the data set. Generally, the mean is a good indicator of the most typical value, and it has the advantage that most people use and understand it. For example, the mean is a good measure of the most typical value of the student marks shown in Table 2.1.

But if there are extreme values, then the median is often better than the mean. Table 2.2 illustrates this well. It shows the land areas of the 45 countries in Europe, which vary in size from the Vatican City, with less than 1 square kilometre, to Russia, with over 17 million square kilometres. In fact, Russia is nearly three times larger than all the other European countries combined. Thus, the mean

(500,000) of the 45 land areas is much larger than the median (65,000) because of the much greater influence of the Russian value on the mean compared to the median.

Table 2.2   Data with a very different mean and median: European states, by land area

State	Area[1]	State	Area	State	Area
Vatican City	0.44	Netherlands	42,000	Bulgaria	110,000
Monaco	2.0	Denmark	44,000	Greece	130,000
Gibraltar	6.5	Estonia	45,000	Belarus	210,000
San Marino	61	Slovakia	49,000	Romania	240,000
Liechtenstein	160	Bosnia–Herzegovina	51,000	UK	250,000
Malta	320	Croatia	57,000	Italy	300,000
Andorra	470	Latvia	65,000	Poland	310,000
Luxembourg	2600	Lithuania	65,000	Norway	320,000
Montenegro	14,000	Ireland	70,000	Finland	340,000
Slovenia	20,000	Czech Republic	79,000	Germany	360,000
Macedonia	25,000	Austria	84,000	Sweden	450,000
Albania	29,000	Serbia	88,000	Spain	500,000
Belgium	31,000	Portugal	92,000	France	550,000
Moldova	34,000	Hungary	93,000	Ukraine	600,000
Switzerland	41,000	Iceland	100,000	Russia	17,000,000

[1]Units are square kilometres (using flexible rounding – see Chapter 6).

Source: Based on data in CIA 2009

BEHIND THE STATS

Russia is by far the biggest country in the world in terms of land area. In fact, it is almost as big as the next two largest (Canada and the USA) *combined* (CIA 2009). For much of the twentieth century it was even bigger. In 1991, the Soviet Union split into Russia and 14 other independent republics. The biggest is Kazakhstan, the world's ninth largest country – but probably better known as the homeland of Borat, the character created by British comedian Sacha Baron Cohen.

As Darrell Huff points out in his classic text *How To Lie With Statistics* (1954: Ch. 2), unscrupulous people can use 'the well-chosen average' deliberately to mislead. And it isn't just the use of the mean or median that you need watch out for. More fundamentally, you can change the most typical value by redefining exactly what it measures. For example, Russia is usually seen as a 'European' country. But the physical and political borders of 'Europe' do not match. In terms of physical geography, most of Russia's land area lies in Asia, not Europe. Without Russia, the mean of the remaining 44 'European' states is less than 140,000 (not 500,000) square kilometres.

A sneaky example of changing the mean by changing what it measures appeared in my daily newspaper recently. For a long time, one television channel had won the 6 p.m. to midnight ratings for the highest mean number of viewers. However, when the channel slipped to second, it promptly changed the measuring period to end at 10.30 p.m. rather than midnight. Its media release then trumpeted that, once again, it had the highest average rating! Look too for the *uninformed* use of such statistics. For example, my local newspaper recently castigated schools because the examination results of half of them fell below the median!

How typical is it?

Once you know the most typical value, the next question is 'How typical is it?' In other words, how good a summary does the mean or median provide? In case you need convincing that this second question actually needs asking, look at the table below, which shows the number of times 14 students from two faculties went to the student bar last week. For example, the first Arts student went 4 times, and the last Science student went 7 times.

Faculty	Number of bar visits	Mean	Median
Arts	4 4 4 4 4 4 4	4	4
Science	1 2 3 4 5 6 7	4	4

As the above table shows, the mean and median of both groups of students are identical. However, although the mean and the median give an excellent description of Arts students, they are not such good measures of Science students. This is because of the bunching of the Arts values (they all went to the bar 4 times), but the wide spread of Science students (from 1 to 7). This is why researchers measure the *spread* of the data around the most typical value – so they can answer the question: '*How typical* is the most typical value?'

As Chapter 1 pointed out, the simplest measure of spread is the *overall range* or the difference between the largest and smallest values. But because the overall range uses the two most extreme values, it's a very crude measure. Instead, researchers use two other statistics, the *midspread* and the *standard deviation*, to measure the spread of the data around the median and mean.

Midspread

The *midspread* measures the spread of the middle 50% of values in a ranked data set. To find the midspread, you identify those values that separate off the middle 50% of values from the smallest 25% and largest 25% of values. The statistic that separates off the lowest one-quarter of values is termed the *lower quartile*, and the statistic that separates off the highest one-quarter of values is the *upper quartile*. The midspread is the difference between these two quartiles, hence its alternative name, the *interquartile range* (Figure 2.2).

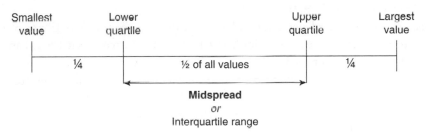

Figure 2.2   Midspread or interquartile range

For example, if you divide the 52 values in Table 2.1 into quarters, there are 13 values in each. The lower quartile separates off the lowest 13 marks from the rest. Table 2.3 shows that the 13th lowest mark is 49 and the 14th lowest is 50. Hence, the value that separates these two marks is half-way between them – 49.5. This is the lower quartile. Similarly, the 13th highest mark is 67 and the 14th is also 67. Hence, the upper quartile is 67. The midspread is simply the difference between the upper quartile (67) and the lower quartile (49.5), which is 17.5 (Figure 2.3).

Table 2.3   Student marks in rank order

28	32	34	34	38	39	41	42	45	46	46	47	49	This row has lowest ¼ of marks
50	51	51	51	52	53	55	55	56	56	56	56	56	
58	58	59	61	63	63	64	65	65	65	66	66	67	
67	69	70	71	71	72	74	75	75	76	84	86	96	This row has highest ¼ of marks

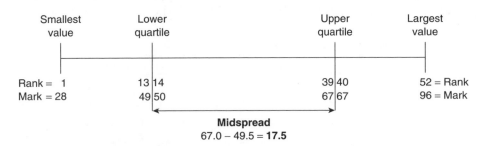

Figure 2.3   Midspread of student marks

Standard deviation

Most of the time, it's the mean rather than the median that's the best measure of the most typical value. To get an idea of how typical the mean is, you need a measure of the spread of the values around it. The *standard deviation* is a measure of the typical difference between each value and the mean.

With anything other than a very small set of values, calculating the standard deviation by hand can be quite time consuming because you have to compare each value with the mean. Thus, rather than using the 52 values from the student marks example, I'll instead show how to calculate the standard deviation using just five values: 2, 4, 7, 8, 9.

Because the standard deviation is based on differences (or deviations) of each value from the mean, not surprisingly the first step is to work out the mean. The sum of the five numbers is 30 (2 + 4 + 7 + 8 + 9), and thus the mean is 6 (30 ÷ 5).

The next step is to work out how much each value differs, or deviates, from the mean. Some of the values (2 and 4) are smaller than the mean, and some (7, 8, and 9) are larger. The mean is a central value – that is why it's regarded as a typical value. So, as the table below shows, if you add all the differences from the mean (−4, −2, +1, +2, +3) you get a total of 0. This is because the negative differences (−4, −2) cancel out the positive differences (+1, +2, +3).

Value	Mean	Difference
2	6	2 − 6 = −4
4	6	4 − 6 = −2
7	6	7 − 6 = +1
8	6	8 − 6 = +2
9	6	9 − 6 = +3
		Sum of differences = 0

In fact, you *always* get zero when you add together these difference values. To get around this, you need to get rid of the minus signs. You could simply ignore the minus signs, but the procedure seems rather dubious (try asking your bank manager to do it!). So, you need another method to get rid of the troublesome minus signs.

There is a mathematical rule that when you multiply two negative numbers, the answer is always positive. Thus, as Table 2.4 shows, when you square a

Table 2.4   Sum of squares

Value	Mean	Actual difference	Squared difference
2	6	−4	−4 × −4 = +16
4	6	−2	−2 × −2 = +4
7	6	+1	+1 × +1 = +1
8	6	+2	+2 × +2 = +4
9	6	+3	+3 × +3 = +9
			Sum of squares = +34

negative value (i.e. multiply it by itself) you get a positive result. If you square the negative differences, you must also square the positive differences. The total (or sum) of these squared differences is the *sum of squares*.

The sum of squares is too influenced by the number of values in the data set for it to be a very useful measure of the spread of the values. For example, normally you'd expect a set of 100 values to have a much larger sum of squares than a data set with only 10 values. The average of the sum of squares, termed the *variance*, is a more useful figure that you can use to compare the spread of values from data sets of any size. As the sum of squares is 34 and there are 5 values, the average of the sum of squares (i.e. the variance) is 6.8:

$$\text{Variance} = \frac{\text{Sum of squares}}{\text{Number of values}} = \frac{34}{5} = 6.8$$

Remember that the variance is the average of the *squared* differences, or deviations. To convert back to the original units – the ones used in the original set of data – you need to find the square root of the variance. This value is the *standard deviation*. As the variance is 6.8, the standard deviation is the square root of 6.8, or 2.6:

$$\text{Standard deviation} = \sqrt{\text{Variance}} = \sqrt{6.8} = 2.6$$

The more spread out the values around the mean, the larger the standard deviation. For example, recall the example about student visits to a bar. The example below adds the Business faculty to the two listed previously:

Faculty	Number of bar visits	Mean	SD
Arts	4 4 4 4 4 4 4	4.0	0.0
Business	2 3 4 4 4 5 6	4.0	1.2
Science	1 2 3 4 5 6 7	4.0	2.0

Every Arts student went to the bar 4 times during the week. Clearly, the mean is 4. The standard deviation (SD) is 0 because there is absolutely no difference between the values and the mean. In contrast, Science students varied widely in how often they went. As a result, although the mean value is still 4, the standard deviation is 2.0. In the middle are the Business students. Their mean value is also 4, but the number of visits varied more than the Arts students but less than the Science students. As a result, the standard deviation for Business students is more than 0 and less than 2.0. The table below shows the steps that you have to go through to calculate the three standard deviations:

Statistic	Arts	Business	Science
Mean	4.0	4.0	4.0
Sum of squares	0.0	10.0	28.0
Variance	0.0	1.4	4.0
Standard deviation	0.0	1.2	2.0

Midspread or standard deviation – which is better?

The preferred measure depends on the earlier decision about whether to use the median or mean. If the median is the measure of the most typical value, then the midspread will show how typical it is. Similarly, if the mean is the measure of the most typical value, then the standard deviation will show how typical it is. The midspread and standard deviation have the same sort of advantages and disadvantages as the associated median and mean:

- Midspread is easier to understand than the standard deviation.
- Midspread is less influenced by extreme values than the standard deviation.
- Standard deviation uses *all* the values, while the midspread uses just ranks for all but those values around the quartiles.
- Standard deviation is more widely used in *hypothesis testing* – where, as Part V at the end of the book shows, you make a hypothesis about a population, and test it using the results from a sample.

This chapter looked at how to measure the most typical value of a numerical variable. The next chapter focuses on categorical variables – that is, characteristics measured using named categories. It shows how to answer the same two basic questions: 'What's the most typical value?' and 'How typical is it?'

THREE

Measuring categories

| Chapter Overview |

This chapter will:

- Emphasise the importance of identifying the overall pattern in a set of categorical data by asking: (I) What's the most typical value? (II) How do the rest of the values spread out around it?
- Outline the difference between working with nominal and ordinal categorical data.
- Show how to find the most typical value using the *mode* with nominal data and the *median* with ordinal data
- Show how to measure the spread of data around the mode using the *variation ratio* and around the median using the *midspread*.

The previous chapter focused on numerical variables. This chapter looks at categorical variables. These are characteristics where the values are in the form of category names. As Chapter 1 pointed out, there are two types of categorical data:

1 Nominal data – where there is no in-built order to the categories.
2 Ordinal data – where there is in-built order to the categories.

Table 3.1 shows six of the many countries of origin of movies included on the Internet Movie Database. The variable is *Country of origin*, and the categories are 'Australia', 'Canada', and so on. There is no built-in order to the categories, and so *Country of origin* is a nominal variable.

Table 3.1   Nominal data: movies, by country of origin

Country	Number
Australia	5830
Canada	20,348
Ireland	1534
New Zealand	896
UK	37,069
USA	237,713

Source: IMDb 2009b

In contrast, Table 3.2 shows the five main categories used to classify films for public exhibition in the UK. The variable is *Exhibition classification*, and the categories are 'Universal', 'Parental guidance', and so on. There is a built-in order to the categories, based on how explicitly a film shows violence, sex, and so on. I'll come back to these two examples throughout the chapter.

Table 3.2   Ordinal data: films approved for public exhibition in UK, by classification

Classification	Explicitness	Number
Universal (abbreviated to 'U')	Very low	69
Parental guidance (PG)	Low	117
Under 12s need accompanying adult (12A)	Medium	178
Under 15s not admitted (15)	High	227
Under 18s not admitted (18)	Very high	48

Source: BBFC 2009

The summary statistics used to describe the distribution of a categorical variable vary slightly depending on whether the level of measurement is nominal or ordinal. However, the two basic questions are the same as with numerical data:

1   What's the most typical value?
2   How typical is it?

Most typical value – nominal data

The previous chapter on numerical data looked at two ways to measure the most typical value: the mean and median. Can they also apply to nominal data?

The mean requires a numerical value for each individual. However, Table 3.1 shows only named categories (e.g. Australia, Canada). Thus, you can't use the mean to measure nominal data. Don't make the mistake of using the numbers in the final column of Table 3.1. Remember, the values are the category names (e.g. UK, USA), one of which is used to describe *each* movie; the numbers (e.g. 37,069) refer to *groups* of movies.

The median requires at least ordinal data. In other words, you need categories that can be ordered in some generally agreed way. But categorical variables at the nominal level of measurement have no built-in order. For example, there is no reason why the countries of origin should always appear in the order shown in Table 3.1.

If you can't use the mean or the median with nominal data, what *can* you use? Basically, not a great deal. The best you can do is identify the category containing the largest number of individuals (i.e. the category with the largest *frequency*). Table 3.1 shows that there are nearly 238,000 movies in the US category. Imagine that you know nothing about the films described in Table 3.1, and have to guess the country of origin of each one. It makes sense to say 'USA' each time, because then you'd be right more often than if you say 'Australia', 'Ireland', or any of the other countries listed. The category containing the largest number of individuals is the *modal category* (or *mode*). In this example, the modal category is 'USA'.

Most typical value – ordinal data

The mean requires a numerical value for each individual, and all categorical variables use category names rather than numbers. Thus, once again you can't use the mean as the most typical value of an ordinal variable. However, you can use the median with ordinal data because the categories can be ordered in some generally agreed way. The categories used to classify films are ordinal, being based on how explicitly a movie shows violence, sex, and so on

---

BEHIND THE STATS

The Story of the Kelly Gang is arguably the first feature-length fiction movie ever produced. It premiered in Melbourne, Australia, in December 1906. Ned Kelly was a 'bushranger' – an outlaw whose gang escaped capture by hiding in the bush, or countryside (see Barry 2006). The movie generated a lot of controversy, with some people seeing it as glorifying criminals. In April 1907, the government 'banned screenings of the film in Kelly's own territory, partly for fear of public disorder and rioting', and later extended the ban throughout the entire state of Victoria (Pike and Cooper 1980: 9).

For example, in the UK film rated 'Universal' are the least explicit, those rated 'Parental guidance' are the second least explicit, and so on. Table 3.3 shows the number of films in each category classified in one year by the British Board of Film Classification (BBFC). In total, there are 639 films.

Table 3.3   Median using ordinal data: films approved for public screening in UK

Classification category	Number	Category ranks	Median rank
Universal (abbreviated to 'U')	69	1–69	
Parental guidance (PG)	117	70–186	
Under 12s need accompanying adult (12A)	178	187–364	320
Under 15s not admitted (15)	227	365–591	
Under 18s not admitted (18)	48	592–639	
Total	**639**	**1–639**	

Source: BBFC 2009

Imagine the 639 films listed according to their BBFC category:

- The first 69 films on the list are rated 'Universal'.
- The next 117 are rated 'Parental guidance'. Thus, the first PG film is 70th on the list, and the last PG film is 186th on the list.
- The next 178 are rated 'Under 12s need accompanying adult' (ranked 187th to 364th on the list).
- The next 227 are rated 'Under 15s not admitted' (ranked 365th to 591st).
- The last 48 films are rated 'Under 18s not admitted' (ranked 592nd to 639th).

You find the rank of the median as follows:

Median rank = ½ × (Number of values in data set + 1)

With 639 films, the film ranked 320th is in the middle of the list, and so the median rank is 320:

Median rank of films = ½ × (Number of films + 1) = ½ × (639+1)
= ½ × 640 = 320

There are 319 films above the median and 319 below it. Table 3.3 shows that the 320th film lies in the 'Under 12s need accompanying adult' category, which includes films ranked 187th to 364th. Thus, the median value for this set of ordered categories is 'Under 12s need accompanying adult'. It's a crude measure, but it's the best you can do with these ordinal data.

The alternative is to use the modal category. In Table 3.3, the category with the greatest number of films is 'Under 15s not admitted'. All in all, the median makes more use of the data than the modal category because it takes into account the ordering of the categories. A general principle of statistical analysis is to squeeze as much information as you can from the data. Using this principle, the median is better than the mode for identifying the most typical value in ordinal data.

How typical is most typical value – nominal data?

With nominal data, you use the modal category to answer the question: 'What is the most typical value?' The next question is 'How typical is the modal category?' You answer this question by calculating the variation ratio. It's the proportion of individuals outside the modal category. You calculate the variation ratio as follows:

$$\text{Variation ratio} = \frac{\text{Individuals outside modal category}}{\text{Total number of individuals}}$$

The less spread out the data, the smaller the proportion of individuals outside the modal category. For example, in Table 3.4 (a) there are 100 individuals spread across five categories (A, B, C, D, E). The modal category is 'C' with 93 individuals. Categories A, B, D, and E together include only 7 individuals. Thus, only 7 of 100 individuals are outside the modal category. Dividing the number outside the modal category (7) by the total number of individuals (100), you can say that the variation ratio is 0.07. Generally, the less spread out the data, the closer the variation ratio comes to zero.

Table 3.4   Variation ratios

(a)						(b)				
Category	A	B	C	D	E	Category	V	W	X	Y	7
Frequency	3	1	93	2	1	Frequency	18	21	22	20	19
Variation ratio – 7 ÷ 100 = 0.07						Variation ratio = 78 ÷ 100 = 0.78					

In contrast, the more spread out the data, the larger the proportion of individuals outside the modal category. For example, in Table 3.4(b) there are 100 individuals spread across five categories (V, W, X, Y, Z). The modal category is 'X' with 22 individuals. The other categories together include the remaining 78 individuals. Dividing the number of individuals outside the modal category (78) by the total number of individuals (100), you can say that the variation ratio is 0.78. Generally, the more spread out the data, the closer the variation ratio comes to 1.0.

Variation ratios usually make most sense when comparing distributions. For example, Table 3.5 shows data about the continental location of each member of the United Nations at two time periods: (i) in 1945, when the UN was set up; and (ii) in 2009. Table 3.5 shows that the variation ratio was 0.55 in 1945 and 0.72 in 2009. This shows that the spread of UN members has become geographically

Table 3.5   Members of United Nations, by continent

(a) In 1945		(b) In 2009	
Continent	Number	Continent	Number
Africa	4	Africa	53
Americas	23	Americas	35
Asia	9	Asia	46
Europe	13	Europe	44
Oceania	2	Oceania	14
Total	**51**	**Total**	**192**

Individuals in modal category (Americas) = 23
Total number of individuals (UN members) = 51
Individuals outside modal category = 51–23 = 28

$$\text{Variation ratio} = \frac{28}{51} = 0.55$$

Individuals in modal category (Africa) = 53
Total number of individuals (UN members) = 192
Individuals outside modal category = 192–53 = 139

$$\text{Variation ratio} = \frac{139}{192} = 0.72$$

Source: Based on UN 2009a

wider over time. Only independent states can be members of the UN, and the change in the variation ratio over time largely reflects the independence of former colonies, particularly in Africa.

How typical is most typical value – ordinal data?

With ordinal data, you use the median to find the most typical value. The next question is 'How typical is the median?' You answer this question by calculating the midspread, though it's a fairly crude measure with categorical data. To illustrate, let's go back to the film ratings in Table 3.3. You calculate the ranks of the lower quartile (cutting off the lowest quarter of values) and upper quartile (cutting off the highest quarter of values) in the usual way. With a total of 639 films, the calculations for the quartile ranks are as follows:

Lower quartile rank = ¼ × (Number of values + 1) = ¼ × 640 = 160th

Upper quartile rank = ¾ × (Number of values + 1) = ¾ × 640 = 480th

Table 3.3 shows that the lower quartile rank (160th) is in the 'Parental guidance' category (which includes films ranked 70th to 186th). The upper quartile rank (480th) is in the 'Under 15s not admitted' category (which includes films ranked 365th to 591st). Thus, the middle 50% of the classified films range between the 'Parental guidance' and 'Under 15s not admitted' categories. This is the best you can do to describe the spread of the data around the median.

This is the final chapter in the measurement part of the book. The following chapter introduces the material about the next part of the book, which is about standardisation.

Part Two

Standardisation

FOUR

Introducing standardisation

Chapter Overview

This chapter will:

- Illustrate how often we all come across standardised data.
- Show how to calculate percentages using categorical data
- Point out the traps associated with using percentages to show changes over time.
- Show how to use *ranks* to standardise numerical data.

The term *standardisation* in this book refers to changing original values to make them easier to understand and compare. Although you may not be familiar with the term, you have certainly come across standardisation many times, and have used it yourself on many occasions. Here are some examples.

Most Australians are aware that over exposure to ultraviolet radiation in sunlight causes permanent skin damage and increases the risk of skin cancer. The Cancer Council of Australia's 'SunSmart' programme (CCA 2009) highlights the fact that Australians have one of the highest rates of skin cancer in the world, nearly four times the rates in Canada, the USA, and the UK. Skin cancer now accounts for over 80% of all cancers diagnosed in Australia. The CCA recommends that people take steps to protect themselves against Sun damage when the ultraviolet index reaches level 3.

These startling facts are *all* based on standardised data. The CCA uses the following types of standardisation:

- *Rates* If you want to compare places which are very different in size, then you need to standardise the original values. If you don't, the comparisons will be at best very difficult and at worst meaningless. For example, the population of Canada is approximately 30 million, the population of the UK is 60 million, and the population of the USA is 300 million. This makes it very difficult to compare the number of people with skin cancer in these countries with the number in Australia where the population is just over 20 million. To make meaningful comparisons, you have to standardise the total number of new cases of skin cancer per so many people (e.g. per 100,000).
- *Ranks* Even the rates per 100,000 may be too detailed. If you need something more basic, you can rank the rates of different countries, from the country with the highest rate (Australia) to the country with the lowest rate.

- *Percentages* This is probably the most common way to standardise data. In this example, over 80 of every 100 new cases of cancer diagnosed in Australia are skin cancers.
- *Indexes* An index measures something that you can't measure directly. Usually it involves combining several different measurements into a single value. The *global solar ultraviolet index* measures the level of risk of skin damage resulting from exposure to the Sun's rays (WHO 2002). The risk depends on a range of factors, including the elevation of the Sun, cloud cover, and altitude, all of which influence the level of UV radiation hitting the ground. The index levels range from 0 (No risk) to 11 (Extreme risk).

We are so familiar with standardised figures that often we are hardly aware that we are dealing with them rather than the original figures. In this example, the original values include the 444,000 Australians who are treated for skin cancer every year. There are two main types, non-melanoma and melanoma skin cancer. Approximately 434,000 people are treated for non-melanoma and more than 10,000 for melanoma skin cancer. Fortunately, non-melanoma skin cancer is much less life threatening: 400 people die every year from non-melanoma and 1200 from melanoma skin cancer. I have spelled out these grim statistics to highlight the difference between standardised values and the original values.

Standardisation techniques vary depending on whether you're dealing with categorical or numerical data. Thus, the following chapters look separately at each type. However, because *percentages* and *ranks* are so widely used with both categorical and numerical data, the remainder of this introductory chapter looks at these.

Percentages

Percentages are probably the most widely used standardisation technique. They often appear in the news media. For example, my daily newspaper tells me that speed cameras deter just 6% of Australian drivers from speeding; that over 40% of patients at Asian hospitals have to pay bribes for medical treatment; and that 96% of cups of tea drunk in the UK are made with teabags. I suspect that the main reason why we come across percentages so often is that they usually fall in the range of 1 to 100, numbers that most people can handle reasonably well.

The basic idea behind percentages is pretty straightforward. A percentage standardises information per 100 (*per centum* is Latin for 'by the 100'). It allows you to compare two numbers by standardising one of them to every 100 units in the other. For example, there are 250 Arts students in a class of 1000 students. What is the percentage of Arts students in the class? Because percentages standardise information per 100, you have to find out how many hundreds of students there are in the class. Clearly, there are 10 lots of 100 in 1000. If the 250 Arts students were divided equally among each of these 10 groups of 100 students, there would be 25 Arts students in each group. In other words, Arts students make up 25% of all students.

In terms of the general structure of the calculation, you need to answer the question: 'What is *this* as a percentage of *that*?' With categorical data, the question expands to 'What is this category frequency as a percentage of that *total frequency?*' The answer to this question comes from the following calculation:

$$\text{Percentage} = \frac{\text{Category frequency}}{\text{Total frequency}} \times 100$$

In the current example, the category is Arts students, and the category frequency is 250. As there are 1000 students altogether, the total frequency is 1000. The percentage calculation now becomes:

$$\text{Percentage} = \frac{\text{Number of Arts students}}{\text{Total number of students}} \times 100 = \frac{250}{1000} \times 100 = 25\%$$

Standardising is particularly useful when comparing patterns over space or time. Table 4.1 illustrates this. Membership of the UN has almost quadrupled from 51 in 1945 to 192 today. This makes it difficult to compare the shift in the continental location of UN members using the original frequency values. In contrast, because they are standardised per 100, percentage figures allow you to compare the relative importance of each continent in 1945 and today. For example, as Table 4.1 shows, the number of African members has gone up from only 8% to 28% of all members.

$$\frac{\% \text{ of African UN}}{\text{members in 1945}} = \frac{\text{Number of African UN members}}{\text{Total number of UN members}} \times 100 = \frac{4}{51} \times 100 = 8\%$$

$$\frac{\% \text{ of African UN}}{\text{members in 2009}} = \frac{\text{Number of African UN members}}{\text{Total number of UN members}} \times 100 = \frac{53}{192} \times 100 = 28\%$$

The data *describe* the shifting pattern of UN membership, but don't *explain* why it has occurred. Often, this is the most difficult part of a research project. In terms of the UN, only politically independent countries are eligible for membership. The changes in UN membership that took place in the second half of the twentieth century reflect the number of former colonies that became independent, especially in Africa.

Table 4.1   UN member states, by continent

(a) In 1945			(b) In 2009		
Continent	Number	%	Continent	Number	%
Africa	4	8	Africa	53	28
Americas	23	45	Americas	35	18
Asia	9	18	Asia	46	24
Europe	13	25	Europe	44	23
Oceania	2	4	Oceania	14	7
Total	**51**	**100**	**Total**	**192**	**100**

Source: Based on UN 2009a

━━━━━━━━━━━━━━ BEHIND THE STATS ━━━━━━━━━━━━━━

Membership of the UN is restricted to independent countries, but includes former colonies that are formally incorporated into the political system of the former colonising power. For example, French Guiana in South America is an integral part of the French Republic. People in French Guiana vote in the French national elections, and their representatives sit in the French Parliament in Paris. Because it is part of France, French Guiana is also part of the European Community. The tiny Caribbean island of Saint Martin is perhaps the most remarkable illustration of the impact of colonialism. Although less than 15 miles (25 kilometres) across, the island was divided by French and Dutch colonialists in the seventeenth century. Today, the northern part (*Saint-Martin*) is an administrative division of France, and the southern part (*Sint Maarten*) is seeking to become an autonomous country within the Kingdom of the Netherlands.

Calculating percentages is usually straightforward with categorical data. However, problems can occur when dealing with numerical data, and particularly when looking at percentage change. The following story, adapted from Dewdney (1993), highlights the misuse of percentages. A student who is down to his last $20 is delighted to find a $10 note, which he promptly puts in his pocket. However, when he gets home he finds that the $10 note has disappeared through a hole in his trouser pocket. But he's not too worried, reasoning that when he found the $10 his wealth went up by 50% (from $20 to $30), whereas when he lost the $10 his wealth went down by only 33% (from $30 to $20), so he's still ahead by 16%! This rather silly example highlights the potential stupidity of adding or subtracting percentages.

Of course, other examples are nothing like as clear cut, and you need to be very careful when dealing with percentage change. Table 4.2 illustrates percentage change.

The final column shows, for example, that between 1950 and 1960 there was a 19.6% increase in world population. To calculate this figure, you first find the increase in population between 1950 and 1960, which is 497 million (3032–2535). You then compare this increase to the original value, which when looking at

Table 4.2   World population

Year	Population total (millions)	Ten-year increase (millions)	Ten-year increase (%)
1950	2535	*	*
1960	3032	3032 − 2535 = 497	$(497 \div 2535) \times 100 = 19.6$
1970	3699	3699 − 3032 = 667	$(667 \div 3032) \times 100 = 22.0$
1980	4451	4451 − 3699 = 752	$(752 \div 3699) \times 100 = 20.3$
1990	5295	5295 − 4451 = 844	$(844 \div 4451) \times 100 = 19.0$
2000	6124	6124 − 5295 = 829	$(829 \div 5295) \times 100 = 15.7$
2010	6909	6909 − 6124 = 785	$(785 \div 6124) \times 100 = 12.8$

* Not shown because base value (1940 population) is unavailable.

Source: Based on UN 2009b

percentage change over time is usually called the *base value*. In this example, therefore, the base value is the 1950 population (2535 million). The percentage calculation works out how many extra people there were in 1960 for every 100 people in 1950. Thus, the population increase between 1950 and 1960 expressed as a percentage of the 1950 population is:

$$\% \text{ increase} = \frac{\text{Increase}}{\text{Base Value}} \times 100 = \frac{\text{Population increase 1950 to 1960}}{\text{Population in 1950}} \times 100$$

$$= \frac{497}{2535} \times 100 = 0.196 \times 100 = 19.6$$

The rest of the percentages in the final column of Table 4.2 are calculated in exactly the same way.

Note that the base value varies with each calculation. For example, the base value is 2535 in the calculation for the 1950 to 1960 increase, and the base value is 6124 for the 2000 to 2010 increase. Because of this, Table 4.2 needs careful interpretation. The final column shows that the percentage increase in population has gone down since 1970. But because the population size has grown throughout the period, a 10% increase in the mid 1950s represents a lot fewer people than a 10% increase in the early 2000s. You have to keep on your toes when looking at percentage change over time.

Because the base value varies with each calculation, you can't meaningfully add the individual percentage values in the final column to give an overall percentage increase between 1950 and 2010. Instead, you need to repeat the basic percentage calculation using (i) the 4374 increase in population between 1950 and 2010, and (ii) the 1950 population (2535) as the base value:

$$\% \text{ increase 1950 to 2010} = \frac{\text{Population increase}}{\text{Population base value}} \times 100 = \frac{4374}{2535} \times 100$$

$$= 1.73 \times 100 = 173$$

Simply adding the percentages in the final column of Table 4.2 gives a total of only 109.4, much smaller than the 173% value. The reason is the changing base values used in the calculation for each of the five decades. It's like trying to add together 19.6 US dollars, 22.0 UK pounds, 20.4 Japanese yen, 18.9 Indian rupees, 15.7 European euros, and 12.8 Russian roubles. You can do it arithmetically, but the answer (109.4 *things*) isn't very meaningful.

Let's focus a bit more on the 173% increase in population. Percentages work best when they are in the range of 0 to 100. Thus, although the calculation is fine, the 173% result is not very helpful. A doubling of values results in a 100% increase, a tripling of values in a 200% increase, and a quadrupling in a 300% increase. These are all percentage values that readers are likely to misinterpret. Thus, rather than describing the total world population as increasing by 173% between 1950 and 2010, a clearer (if less precise) description is that the world population almost tripled between 1950 and 2010. It's a good idea to confine percentages to changes of less than 100%.

Ranks

Another widely used standardisation procedure is to rank individuals (sometimes categories) from best to worst, or highest to lowest. I'm writing the first draft of this chapter at the start of a new year, and the media are filled with stories about the top 10 movies, music albums, video clips, TV programmes, books, and so on. The ranking technique is widely used because it is simple to understand and, like percentages, produces numbers that range from 1 to 100.

For example, Table 4.3 ranks movies in terms of their box office takings (i.e. the value of all cinemas tickets sold). It shows that *Titanic* took an incredible $1840 million at the box office to be the most popular movie ever. Thus, *Titanic* is ranked number 1; *Lord of the Rings: The Return of the King* is ranked number 2, taking $1130 million at the box office; and *Pirates of the Caribbean: Dead Man's Chest* is ranked number 3, taking $1060 million. Incidentally, when looking at dollar values over time, it's always useful to see if they have been standardised for inflation, as a dollar or pound can buy much less now than it could 10 years ago, and *very* much less than 20 years ago. The dollar values in Table 4.3 are not adjusted for inflation. This explains why so many of the top 10 movies have recent release dates.

Table 4.3   Most successful movies, by worldwide box office takings

Title (release date)	Takings[1]	Rank
Titanic (1997)	$1840	1
Lord of the Rings: The Return of the King (2003)	$1130	2
Pirates of the Caribbean: Dead Man's Chest (2006)	$1060	3
Dark Knight (2008)	$1002	4
Harry Potter and the Sorcerer's Stone (2001)	$969	5
Pirates of the Caribbean: At World's End (2007)	$958	6
Harry Potter and the Order of the Phoenix (2007)	$937	7
Star Wars: Phantom Menace (1999)	$922	8.5
Lord of the Rings: The Two Towers (2002)	$922	8.5
Jurassic Park (1993)	$920	10

[1] Box office takings only, in millions of US dollars. Figures not adjusted for inflation.

Source: Based on data in IMDb 2009a

An online reporting service gives the following prices for US cinema tickets: 2009, $7.18; 1989, $3.97; 1969, $1.42; 1949, $0.46; 1929, $0.35 (Box Office Mojo 2009). After adjusting for inflation, *Gone with the Wind* (released 1939), *Snow White and the Seven Dwarfs* (1937), and the first *Star Wars* movie (1977) are likely to give *Titanic* a close run as the most commercially successful movie ever. However, in terms of marketing, film studios prefer using unadjusted figures so that they can announce new box office 'records'.

What happens when two or more of the original values are identical? Notice that the 1999 *Star Wars* movie and the 2002 *Lord of the Rings* movie took equal amounts at the box office ($922 million). It makes sense to give equal values an equal rank – and so these films both have a rank of 8.5. I'll use the simple example below to explain how the tied ranking system works:

Value	100	90	80	80	70	60	60	60	50
Rank	1	2	3.5	3.5	5	=7	=7	=7	9

The highest value (100) has a rank of 1 and the second highest (90) a rank of 2. The two 80 values are ranked 3.5, the average of 3 and 4, the ranks they would be if the two values were slightly different (e.g. 81 and 80). The next value (70) has a rank of 5, the same as if all the larger values were different. Similarly, the three 60 values have the same rank of 7, the average of 6, 7, and 8. Consequently, the next value (50) is ranked 9, the same as if all the larger values were different. A good check on the accuracy of your rankings is to see if the lowest rank is the same as the number of values. The only time this is not the case is when there is more than one bottom-ranking value.

This chapter introduced the idea of standardisation. The following two chapters look at standardisation in more detail. Chapter 5 focuses on categorical variables, and Chapter 6 focuses on numerical variables.

Five

Standardising categories

Chapter Overview

This chapter will:

- Recap earlier comments about using *percentages* with categorical data.
- Show how to calculate *proportions*.
- Show how to calculate *ratios*.
- Illustrate how percentages, proportions, and ratios can be misleading. In these circumstances, *rates of occurrence* can give more meaningful results.

Recall that the term *standardisation* refers to changing original values to make them easier to understand and compare. The previous chapter introduced standardisation. This chapter recaps some of the earlier comments about percentages, and then looks at some of the other ways to standardise categorical data: proportions, ratios, and rates of occurrence.

Percentages

A percentage standardises information per 100. It allows you to compare two numbers by standardising one of them to every 100 units in the other. For example, there are 250 Arts students in a class of 1000 students. What is the percentage of Arts students in the class? Because percentages standardise information per 100, you have to find out how many hundreds of students there are in the class. Clearly, there are 10 lots of 100 in 1000. If the 250 Arts students were divided equally among each of these 10 groups of 100 students, there would be 25 Arts students in each group. In other words, Arts students make up 25% of all students. This line of reasoning is reflected in the following calculation:

$$\text{Percentage} = \frac{\text{Category frequency}}{\text{Total frequency}} \times 100$$

In the current example, the category is Arts students, and the category frequency is 250. As there are 1000 students altogether, the total frequency is 1000. The percentage calculation now becomes:

$$\text{Percentage} = \frac{\text{Number of Arts students}}{\text{Total number of students}} \times 100 = \frac{250}{1000} \times 100 = 25\%$$

Table 5.1 shows several real-world percentage calculations. For example, Table 5.1(b) shows that 44 of the 192 UN members are in Europe. The result of the percentage calculation shows that 23 of every 100 UN members are in Europe. In other words, 23% of UN members are European countries. This figure is very similar to the European percentage for 1945 (25%), despite membership of the UN having almost quadrupled. What the percentage figures do not tell you is that several European countries in existence in 1945, in particular the Soviet Union and Yugoslavia, later divided into smaller independent states, and then became UN members.

Table 5.1   Percentages: UN members, by continent, 1945 and 2009

(a) In 1945			(b) In 2009		
Continent	Number	%	Continent	Number	%
Africa	4	$(4 \div 51) \times 100 = 8$	Africa	53	$(53 \div 192) \times 100 = 28$
Americas	23	$(23 \div 51) \times 100 = 45$	Americas	35	$(35 \div 192) \times 100 = 18$
Asia	9	$(9 \div 51) \times 100 = 18$	Asia	46	$(46 \div 192) \times 100 = 24$
Europe	13	$(13 : 51) \times 100 = 25$	Europe	44	$(44 \div 192) \times 100 = 23$
Oceania	2	$(2 \div 51) \times 100 = 4$	Oceania	14	$(14 \div 192) \times 100 = 7$
Total	**51**	**100**	**Total**	**192**	**100**

Source: Based on UN 2009a

Proportions

You can standardise by any number you want; it doesn't *have* to be 100. For example, you could use the *permillage* system, and standardise by 1000 (*mille* is Latin for thousand). There is even a permillage symbol (‰). However, this system has not caught on, mainly I suspect because it requires working with numbers up to 999 – which are too large for many people.

Of course, you could go the other way, and standardise to less than 100. For example, 10 seems a nice round number. But such a system is likely to be too crude for many situations, unless you add a decimal point – which spoils the simplicity. However, the use of *proportions* is common in statistics. This system involves standardising 'per 1' or 'per unit'. Calculate a proportion exactly as for a percentage, but without the final multiplication by 100:

$$\text{Proportion} = \frac{\text{Category frequency}}{\text{Total frequency}}$$

For example, there are 44 UN members in Europe out of a total of 192 UN members. Thus, the proportion of UN members located in Europe is:

$$\text{Proportion of European UN members} = \frac{\text{European UN members}}{\text{All UN members}} = \frac{44}{192} = 0.23$$

Table 5.2 shows this and other proportion values. Proportions are commonplace in statistics books, and it's important to be aware of them. However, you rarely find proportions anywhere else, mainly because proportions lie well outside the 1 to 100 comfort zone of many people.

Table 5.2   Percentages, proportions, and ratios: UN member states, by continent, 2009

Continent	Number	%	Proportion	Ratio
Africa	53	28	0.28	1 in 3.6
Americas	35	18	0.18	1 in 5.5
Asia	46	24	0.24	1 in 4.2
Europe	44	23	0.23	1 in 4.4
Oceania	14	7	0.07	1 in 13.7
Total	**192**	**100**	**1.00**	**1 in 1**

Source: Based on UN 2009a

BEHIND THE STATS

One exception of proportions not being used in the mass media is tables of standings in US sports. For example, basketball fans would immediately understand that 0.500 shows that their team had won half of its matches. However, in a standings table, the column showing proportions is usually headed 'Pct', for Percentage. And the proportion is usually referred to as a whole number – for example, 'I'm pleased my team has reached 500 in the standings'.

Ratios

At times, the level of detail provided by percentages and proportions is more than you really need. For example, you might say that approximately 1 in 4 UN members are Asian states. These are *ratios*. A ratio shows how many individuals there are in the total for every one in a particular category. Calculate a ratio as follows:

$$\text{Ratio} = 1 \text{ in } \frac{\text{Total frequency}}{\text{Category frequency}}$$

For example, there are 46 UN members in the category 'Asia' out of a total of 192 UN members. Thus, the ratio of UN members located in Asia is:

$$\text{Ratio of Asian states} = 1 \text{ in } \frac{\text{All UN members}}{\text{Asian UN members}} = 1 \text{ in } \frac{192}{46} = 1 \text{ in } 4.2$$

You often see ratios presented as whole numbers in sentences. Thus, you are likely to describe the 1 in 4.2 ratio as 'just over 1 in 4 UN members are from Asia'. The *Ratio* column of Table 5.2 shows the ratios for all continents.

Rates of occurrence

Percentages, proportions, and ratios can sometimes be misleading. For example, one column of Table 5.3 shows the number of traffic fatalities in 15 European countries; the next column shows the associated percentage values. Over three-quarters (77.1%) of all fatalities occur in just five countries: Italy, Germany, France, Spain, and the UK. On the other side of the coin, less than one-quarter (22.9%) of all fatalities occur in the other 10 countries.

The impression given by these percentages is that the roads in Italy, Germany, France, Spain, and the UK are much more dangerous than roads elsewhere in

Table 5.3 Percentages and rates of occurrence: West European states, road fatalities

Country	Number	%	Rate[1]
Austria	730	2.5	88
Belgium	1069	3.5	101
Denmark	306	1.1	56
Finland	336	1.2	64
France	4709	17.2	77
Germany	5091	17.3	62
Greece	1657	5.2	149
Ireland	368	1.3	86
Italy	5669	17.5	96
Luxembourg	36	0.1	76
Netherlands	730	2.4	45
Portugal	969	4.0	92
Spain	4104	14.3	93
Sweden	445	1.4	49
UK	3297	10.8	54
Total	**29,516**	**100**	**79**

[1] Rate per million population.

Source: Based on EURF 2008: 44 and 46

Western Europe. But there are more people – and thus more traffic – in these countries, and you might expect that the more traffic there is, the more traffic accidents there will be.

You can avoid such misleading conclusions by using a *rate of occurrence*. The major difference between this and the other statistics in this chapter is that rates of occurrence bring a second variable into the calculations. For example, you can standardise the number of traffic fatalities in each country by its total population, thus getting over the problem that countries vary greatly in size. For example, in the UK, 3297 people out of a total population of just over 60 million were killed in road accidents. Thus, the UK's rate of occurrence is as follows:

$$\text{UK rate of occurrence} = \frac{\text{UK traffic fatalities}}{\text{UK population}} = \frac{3297}{60,587,000} = 0.000054$$

This rate is much too small to be readily understandable. The way to get around the problem is to express the rate of occurrence as a 'rate per so many', the *so many* being whatever number provides a readily understandable set of figures. For example:

$$\text{UK rate of occurrence per hundred population} = \frac{3297}{60,587,000} \times 100 = 0.0054$$

$$\text{UK rate of occurrence per thousand population} = \frac{3297}{60,587,000} \times 1000 = 0.054$$

$$\text{UK rate of occurrence per hundred thousand population} = \frac{3297}{60,587,000} \times 100,000 = 5.4$$

$$\text{UK rate of occurrence per million population} = \frac{3297}{60,587,000} \times 1,000,000 = 54$$

The rates of occurrence per hundred and per thousand population still produce values that are much less than 1, and thus are too small to be readily understandable. In contrast, the rate per 100,000 is 5.4, and the rate per million population is 54, both of which fall within the preferred range of 1 to 100. Table 5.3 uses the rate per million to show road fatalities for 15 West European countries.

Clearly, the rate per million population shows a very different picture from the original percentages. This is because the rates are not affected by the very different population totals between countries. For example, the UK has relatively safe roads, with a rate of 54 deaths per million population, and Germany is not far behind (62). In contrast, both countries with fatality rates over 100 per million have relatively small populations (and thus have quite small percentage values).

Table 5.3 shows that Greece stands out as the country with the most dangerous roads, with a fatality rate of 149 per million population, more than twice that of Germany.

BEHIND THE STATS

An Irish politician has suggested that Ireland should give up driving on the left-hand side of the road to reduce accidents by foreigners used to driving on the right. In Europe, only the UK and Ireland still drive on the left. Sweden was the last European state to change from left to right, in 1967. The main reason why the right-hand side became the standard across Europe was that Napoleon decreed that conquered countries use the same side of the road as France. Similarly, largely because of the global extent of the British Empire, worldwide about one-third of drivers use the left-hand side. There is little evidence that driving on the left was ever widespread among British colonies in America. In Canada, however, British Columbia and the Atlantic provinces switched to the right in the 1920s, and Newfoundland switched in 1949 when it joined Canada. See Lucas (2005) and Kincaid (1986).

This chapter focused on standardising categorical variables. The next, Chapter 6, looks at ways to standardise numerical variables. The chapter starts with simplifying original values, then recaps and develops some earlier comments about using ranks, and finally looks at two more specialised techniques.

SIX

Standardising numbers

| **Chapter Overview** |

This chapter will:
- Basically show how to standardise numerical information to make it easy to understand and compare.
- Show how to simplify numbers by converting and *rounding* units.
- Recap *ranking* and show how to use *percentile ranks*.
- Explain why *standard scores* are useful, and show how to calculate them.
- Illustrate the use of *indexes* and show how to construct one.

Recall that the term *standardisation* refers to changing original values to make them easier to understand and compare. Chapter 5 looked at ways to standardise categorical data. This chapter focuses on standardising numerical data. Measuring with numbers usually means that there are many more unique values than occur with categorical variables, where you place the units of analysis into only a handful of categories. In addition, you can manipulate numbers in ways that are impossible with named categories. The chapter starts with simplifying original values, then recaps and develops some earlier comments about using ranks, and finally looks at two more specialised techniques, standard scores and indexes.

Simplifying original values

This section looks at two often interrelated techniques, *conversion of units* and *rounding*. The basic aim is to make complex numbers easier to understand, use, and remember, ideally by standardising them so that they come within the range of 1 to 100. The downside is that each value becomes less precise, though often this may not matter as we usually need a headline figure (e.g. 'Man wins $1 million') rather than an exact figure (e.g. A man wins $1,020,407).

The *Number* column of Table 6.1 shows the number of barrels of oil consumed every day in different parts of the world. These values are too large to mean very much to the average reader. To reduce the size of the numbers, the next column shows oil consumption in *thousands* of barrels. This helps, but the numbers are still too large, and so the next column shows *millions* of barrels. This is better, the values ranging from about 20 to less than 1. However, each value has far too many digits for most people to deal with comfortably. As this level of detail is not necessary for reading the table, it's useful to round off each value.

Table 6.1   Converting and rounding units: oil consumption, barrels per day

Country/bloc	Number	Thousands	Millions (unrounded)	Millions (fixed rounding)[1]	Millions (variable rounding)[2]
USA	20,680,000	20,680.0	20.6800	21	21.00
EU	14,380,000	14,380.0	14.3800	14	14.00
China	7,880,000	7880.0	7.8800	8	7.90
Japan	5,007,000	5007.0	5.0070	5	5.00
India	2,722,000	2722.0	2.7220	3	2.70
Russia	2,699,000	2699.0	2.6990	3	2.70
Brazil	2,372,000	2372.0	2.3720	2	2.40
Canada	2,371,000	2371.0	2.3710	2	2.40
Australia	966,200	966.2	0.9662	1	0.97
New Zealand	158,400	158.4	0.1584	0	0.16

[1] Rounding to nearest million barrels.
[2] Rounding to two digits.

Source: Based on data in CIA 2009

Table 6.1 shows two columns of rounded data. The *fixed rounding* column shows the millions of barrel of oil rounded to whole numbers. You do this as follows:

- If the digit immediately after the decimal point is a 0, 1, 2, 3, or 4, then the digit before the decimal point remains the same (e.g. 14.<u>3</u>800 rounds to 14).
- If the digit immediately after the decimal point is a 5, 6, 7, 8, or 9, then the digit before the decimal point goes up (e.g. 20.<u>6</u>800 rounds to 21).

This is *fixed* rounding because the rounding rules are fixed regardless of the size of the value. The fixed rounding values are clearer than the unrounded values, but there are still problems. For example, the rounding is too crude for countries in the bottom half of the list, especially New Zealand, which has a nonsensical value of 0.

Another approach is to use *variable rounding*, as shown in the final column of Table 6.1. (The term *variable* rounding contrasts with *fixed* rounding.) In variable rounding, you usually round each value to the first two (occasionally three) digits, regardless of the number of digits. For example, the US value is 20.6800. Focus on the first two digits (20) and round up only when the following digit is a 5, 6, 7, 8, or 9. Thus, round up 20.<u>6</u>800… to 21. So far, variable rounding doesn't seem much different from fixed rounding. But when you use the same technique with the smaller values, you can see the difference between the two techniques. For example, the New Zealand value is 0.1584. Again, focus on the first two digits (15) and round up only if the following digit is a 5, 6, 7, 8, or 9. Thus, round 15<u>8</u>4… up to **16** because the third digit in the original value is <u>8</u>. The New Zealand value on the table is thus 0.16. Similarly, the India value (2.7<u>2</u>20) rounds down to 2.7, and the Russia value (2.6<u>9</u>90) rounds up to 2.7. The advantage of variable rounding is that it leaves some detail of the original value regardless of its absolute size.

The values produced by variable rounding shown on Table 6.1 are a big improvement on the original number of barrels. They show just how useful it can be to standardise data through: (i) the conversion of units; and (ii) rounding. These simple standardisation techniques make the information as easy as possible to understand, use, and remember.

Ranks and percentile ranks

Undoubtedly, the most widely used standardisation procedure for numerical variables is simply to *rank* individuals from best to worst or highest to lowest. It is no surprise that one of the simplest techniques is also the most widely used. Chapter 4 looked at ranking, using the data shown again here as Table 6.2, which ranks movies in terms of their box office takings (i.e. the value of all cinema tickets sold). *Titanic* is ranked number 1, taking $1840 million at the box office to be the most popular movie ever. And *Lord of the Rings: The Return of the King* is ranked number 2, taking $1130 million.

When dealing with a large number of values, often you don't need the precise ranking of an individual. In these circumstances, use *percentile ranks* by grouping the ranked values into 100 equal parts and identifying each part by its rank. The lowest 1% of values has a percentile rank of 1; the highest 1% of values has a percentile rank of 100. For example, imagine the numbers 1 to 1000 in a long line. To divide the 1000 numbers into 100 equal parts, you need 10 numbers in each

Table 6.2   Ranks: movies, by worldwide box office takings

Title (release date)	Takings[1]	Rank
Titanic (1997)	$1840	1
Lord of the Rings: The Return of the King (2003)	$1130	2
Pirates of the Caribbean: Dead Man's Chest (2006)	$1060	3
Dark Knight (2008)	$1002	4
Harry Potter and the Sorcerer's Stone (2001)	$969	5
Pirates of the Caribbean: At World's End (2007)	$958	6
Harry Potter and the Order of the Phoenix (2007)	$937	7
Star Wars: Phantom Menace (1999)	$922	=8.5
Lord of the Rings: The Two Towers (2002)	$922	=8.5
Jurassic Park (1993)	$920	10

[1] Box office takings only, in millions of US dollars. Figures not adjusted for inflation.

Source: Based on data in IMDb 2009a

part. The bottom 1% of values (values 1 to 10) have a percentile rank of 1, the second lowest 1% of values (values 11 to 20) have a percentile rank of 2, and so on up to the top 1% of values (values 991 to 1000) which have a percentile rank of 100. For example, Table 6.3 shows that the value 17 has a percentile rank of 2, and the value 985 has a percentile rank of 99.

Table 6.3   Percentile ranks: a thousand values from 1 to 1000

Percentile rank 1	Percentile rank 2	...	Percentile rank 50	...	Percentile rank 99	Percentile rank 100
1	11	...	491	...	981	991
2	12	...	492	...	982	992
3	13	...	493	...	983	993
4	14	...	494	...	984	994
5	15	...	495	...	985	995
6	16	...	496	...	986	996
7	17	...	497	...	987	997
8	18	...	498	...	988	998
9	19	...	499	...	989	999
10	20	...	500	...	990	1000

Calculate a percentile rank as follows:

$$\text{Percentile rank} = \frac{\text{Actual rank}}{\text{Maximum rank}} \times 100$$

For example, if you have the 8590th highest score in a public exam involving a total of 8760 students, your percentile rank is:

$$\text{Percentile rank} = \frac{\text{Actual rank}}{\text{Maximum rank}} \times 100 = \frac{8590}{8760} \times 100 = 98$$

If you have a percentile rank of 98, then 98% of examinees have a score equal to or less than your score. You'd probably prefer to turn that around and say that only 2% of students have higher scores.

Percentiles divide a set of ranked data into 100 equal parts. You may also come across other similar systems for dividing a ranked set of values. For example, Chapter 2 looked at *quartiles*, which divide ranked values into four equal parts:

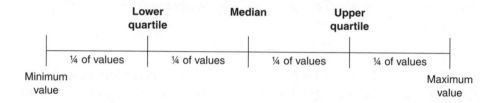

Similarly, *quintiles* divide ranked values into five equal parts (each with 20% of all values), and *deciles* divide ranked values into ten equal parts (each with 10% of all values). You often see quintiles and deciles used to describe the distribution of wealth and income. Table 6.4 shows data collected by various national statistical agencies about how household income varies between quintile groups. For example, in the USA, households in the poorest quintile (the poorest 20% of households) have 3% of all income; households in the richest quintile have 51% of all income. As each quintile includes 20% of households, the more the income figures differ from a 20/20/20/20/20 split, the more unequal is the distribution of income. Look out for percentiles, quartiles, quintiles, and deciles in your reading.

Table 6.4   Quintiles: households, by income quintiles

Quintile	Australia	UK	USA
Poorest	7	6	3
Second	13	11	9
Third	18	16	15
Fourth	23	22	23
Richest	39	44	51

Sources: ABS 2007; Jones 2008; USCB 2008b

Standard scores

Ranks are easy to calculate and easy to understand. However, when standardising with ranks, you lose a lot of the information contained in the original values. To use some of the jargon from Chapter 2, you go from an *interval* level of measurement to an *ordinal* level of measurement. For example, recall Table 6.2 about the world's most commercially successful movies. Box office takings are at the interval level of measurement – so called because you can measure the *interval* (or difference) between values. For example, *Titanic* took $710 million more than *The Return of the King*, and *The Two Towers* took $2 million more than *Jurassic Park*. But when you simplify these dollar values to ranks, all you can now say is *Titanic* took more than *The Return of the King*, and that *The Two Towers* took more than *Jurassic Park*. The fact that 'more' means $710 million in the first pair of movies, and $2 million in the second pair, is lost in the rankings.

In contrast to ranks, standard scores (or *z-scores*) are not quite as straightforward to calculate or understand, but do retain all the original information. Standard scores measure how far each value differs, or deviates, from the mean. You then compare this deviation to the standard deviation. Look back to Chapter 2 if you need to remind yourself about standard deviations.

For example, the 52 student marks below have a mean of 58.2 and a standard deviation of 14.3. The mean is the starting point for standard scores and, like most starting points, it has a value of 0. The standard deviation is the measuring unit (a 'standard deviation unit') against which you compare the deviation of each individual value from the mean.

32	74	63	51	51	96	69	52	42	70	56	84	41
53	65	65	39	46	63	51	55	58	75	50	75	76
46	34	64	71	66	47	28	71	55	56	56	67	66
56	34	86	38	72	61	65	56	58	59	49	45	67

Mean = 58.2, Standard deviation = 14.3

For example, a mark of 72.5 is 14.3 above the mean (72.5 – 58.2 = 14.3). As each standard deviation unit is worth 14.3 marks, then 72.5 is one standard deviation unit above the mean. Thus, in this data set an original value of 72.5 has a standard score of +1, the plus sign showing that the score is *above* the mean. Similarly, a value of 43.9 is 14.3 below the mean (58.2 – 14.3 = 43.9), or one standard deviation unit below the mean. Thus, as the diagram below shows, in this data set an original value of 43.9 has a standard score of −1, the minus sign showing that the score is less than the mean:

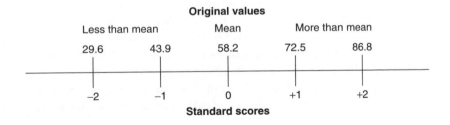

The following points recap the above comments about standard scores:

- Original values that are the same as the mean have a standard score of 0.
- Those original values with an average deviation, or standard deviation, from the mean have a standard score of 1.
- The bigger the deviation of an original value from the mean, the bigger its standard score.
- Original values that are more than the mean have positive standard scores.
- Original values that are less than the mean have negative standard scores.
- Calculate a standard score as follows:

$$\frac{\text{Original value} - \text{Mean}}{\text{Standard deviation}}$$

Because these characteristics always apply, you can directly compare sets of standardised data. For example, Jessica has a mark of 65 in Sociology and 70 in Psychology. Has she done better at Sociology or Psychology? In absolute terms, she has done better in Psychology – 70 is higher than 65. But how has she done in relation to all the other students in each course? The following figures give the information you need to standardise the scores, and thus make a more meaningful comparison:

	Sociology	Psychology
Jessica's mark	65	70
Mean mark	55	65
Standard deviation	5	10

Jessica's standard score in Sociology is +2.0:

$$\frac{\text{Jessica's Sociology}}{\text{standard score}} = \frac{\text{Original value} - \text{Mean}}{\text{Standard deviation}} = \frac{65-55}{5} = \frac{10}{5} = +2.0$$

And her standard score in Psychology is +0.5:

$$\frac{\text{Jessica's Psychology}}{\text{standard score}} = \frac{\text{Original value} - \text{Mean}}{\text{Standard deviation}} = \frac{70-65}{10} = \frac{5}{10} = +0.5$$

The two plus signs show that she has done better than average in both Sociology and Psychology. But despite the higher absolute mark in Psychology, her standard scores show that, relative to all the other students in each course, she has done much better in Sociology (**+2.0**) than in Psychology (**+0.5**).

Lecturers often standardise marks. They do this because they believe that although student ability remains constant from year to year, tests may vary in their degree of difficulty, and staff may vary in their marking standards. Standardisation ensures that overall student marks do not vary from year to year.

For example, every year lecturers teaching a social statistics course standardise student marks to a mean of 60 and a standard deviation of 10. The actual marks this year show a mean of 65 and a standard deviation of 5. To standardise this year's marks, the lecturers first have to convert all the original marks into standard scores. For example, Michael has a mark of 77.5. His standard score is +2.5:

$$\text{Michael's standard score} = \frac{\text{Original mark} - \text{Mean mark}}{\text{Standard deviation}} = \frac{77.5 - 65}{5} = \frac{12.5}{5} = +2.5$$

Thus, Michael's original mark is 2.5 standard deviation units above the mean. The lecturers want to standardise student marks to a mean of 60 and a standard deviation of 10. In this new scheme, Michael's revised mark will still be 2.5 standard deviations more than the specified mean – in other words, 2.5 'lots' of 10, or 25 marks, above 60. Thus, Michael's standardised mark is 85% (25 + 60). More generally, the lecturers standardise their students' marks as follows:

Standardised mark = Specified mean + (Standard score × Specified standard deviation)

For example:

Michael's standardised mark = 60 + (2.5 × 10) = 60 + 25 = 85

Indexes

Most people like lists, and the media are full of them. For example, *Forbes* magazine is famous for its lists. They include the 'world's 100 most powerful women', currently headed by Angela Merkel, the German Chancellor (Egan and Schoenberger 2008), and the 'world's 100 most powerful celebrities', currently headed by Angelina Jolie (Miller et al. 2009).

Of course, *power* is a concept that you can't measure directly, like height or eye colour. A multifaceted concept that you can measure only by combining several simpler concepts is called a *construct*. Commercial list-makers, like *Forbes* magazine, are usually rather vague about how they generate the lists – after all, they don't want competitors copying them. But when you look at any research about a multifaceted concept, always try to find as much information as you can about how the researchers have measured it. If they have included the wrong things and/or missed out some of the right things, then the work will not be *valid*. In other words, it will not measure what it is intended to measure.

To show how to measure a multifaceted concept, I'll use the familiar example of the best car awards given by motoring organisations. The construct *Best family car* is not something researchers can measure directly. Instead, they have to make sure that they take into account all the big things a typical buyer looks for. These are likely to include value for money, safety, and drivability. These 'big things' are *dimensions*. Each dimension then needs breaking into smaller parts. For example, 'value for money' will include sale price, depreciation, fuel consumption, warranty, and so on. These more specific things are *indicators*. The final step is to find a way to measure each indicator. For example, you can measure fuel consumption in miles per gallon or litres per 100 kilometres. These are the *variables*. A car might have a fuel consumption of 24 miles per gallon (or 10 litres per 100 kilometres). These are the *values*. Table 6.5 shows the basic procedure for constructing an index.

Table 6.5   Creating an index

	↗	**Indicator A**	→	Variable 1	→	Value 1
Dimension 1	→	**Indicator B**	→	Variable 2	→	Value 2
	↘	**Indicator C**	→	Variable 3	→	Value 3
	↗	**Indicator D**	→	Variable 4	→	Value 4
Dimension 2	→	**Indicator E**	→	Variable 5	→	Value 5
	↘	**Indicator F**	→	Variable 6	→	Value 6
	↗	**Indicator G**	→	Variable 7	→	Value 7
Dimension 3	→	**Indicator H**	→	Variable 8	→	Value 8
	↘	**Indicator I**	→	Variable 9	→	Value 9
		Index = all measured values combined				

BEHIND THE STATS

France was the first country to officially adopt the metric system, during the period of the French Revolution (1789–99). The new unit of length, the metre, was one ten-millionth of the distance from the North Pole to the equator along a line of longitude running through France. Today, all but three countries (USA, Liberia, Burma) have officially adopted the metric system (see USMA 2009). French revolutionary zeal also led to a short-lived experiment with metric time: each day had 10 hours; each hour had 100 minutes; and each minute had 100 seconds. In 1786, the USA became the first country to use a decimal currency. Today, all but two countries (Madagascar and Mauretania) have decimal currencies.

Once researchers identify the variables and collect the data, the next stage is to combine values from all the variables into a single figure. This is an *index*. To do this, all the values need to be in the same units. But it's very likely that the variables will be in very different units. For example, you might measure the variable Warranty by number of years (e.g. 3) and the variable Fuel consumption in miles per gallon (e.g. 24 mpg). However, it does not make sense simply to add the two values (e.g. 3 years + 24 mpg does not equal 27!).

The simplest way to combine values from variables measured in very different units is to *rank* all cars on each variable, and then add the rank scores to provide an overall index. For example, Table 6.6 shows how eight cars (A to H) compare on the construct *Best family car*, measured using three dimensions, each dimension measured by three variables. Values for each variable have been standardised using ranks.

Table 6.6   Index for 'Best family car'

Car	Dimension 1			Dimension 2			Dimension 3			Index[2]	Index rank
	Var 1[1]	Var 2	Var 3	Var 4	Var 5	Var 6	Var 7	Var 8	Var 9		
A	3	4	3	3	3	3	5	7	4	35	3
B	4	5	5	6	7	4	2	5	5	43	4
C	1	3	2	1	2	1	4	2	2	18	1
D	7	6	4	5	4	8	3	4	6	47	5
E	8	7	6	4	5	7	6	6	3	52	6
F	2	8	7	8	6	2	7	8	8	56	8
G	5	2	1	2	1	5	1	1	1	19	2
H	6	1	8	7	8	6	8	3	7	54	7

[1] Columns show ranking of cars on each variable. Best car = 1.
[2] Each car's index is sum of ranks in each *row*. Best = lowest index.

For example, Variable 1 is Retail price. The Variable 1 column in Table 6.6 shows that Car C scores best, and so ranks 1, Car F scores second best and ranks 2, and so on. Similarly, Variable 2 is Repair costs. The Variable 2 column in Table 6.6 shows that Car H scores best, and so ranks 1, Car G scores second best and ranks 2, and so on. Because all the values in the body of the table are ranks, you can legitimately add together the ranks for each car in all nine columns. For example, Car A ranks third for Variable 1, fourth for Variable 2, third for Variable 3, and so on, giving a total score of 35. This is the index score for that car. It shows how well it has done overall relative to the other cars.

However, the index scores themselves are usually much less important than the rankings of the index scores, which are in the final column of Table 6.6. Because of the ranking procedure, the best score is the lowest one. In this example the best possible score is 9, which occurs only if a car is ranked first for all nine variables. And the worst possible score is 72, the result of a car being last (i.e. ranked eighth) for all nine variables. The final column of Table 6.6 shows that Car C takes the *Best family car* award, closely followed by Car G.

You may have wondered about the scoring of the *Best family car* index because simply adding the ranks from all nine variables assumes that all variables are equally important. This is unlikely to be true, of course. For example, buyers might regard price as critical to their choice of car, whereas a car's quietness has much lower importance. When developing indexes to measure constructs, researchers often do surveys to assess public opinion about how they feel about the importance of each feature. For example, new car buyers might say that price is twice as important as quietness. Using this survey result, researchers will make scores from the price variable twice as important as scores for the quietness variable when calculating their *Best family car* index. This is called *weighting*.

A real-world example of weighting is the development of the *Times Higher Education*–QS World University Rankings (THES-QS 2009). Harvard University currently heads the list. There are five dimensions to the index: (i) academic peer review (weighted at 40% of the total index); (ii) staff–student ratio (20%); (iii) citations per member of staff (20%); (iv) employer review (10%); and (v) proportion of international staff and students (10%). Clearly, the choice of dimensions is open to debate, as are the weightings. When you come across indexes in your reading, always see if the researchers have used weightings. If they haven't, then ask if they have evidence to allow them to treat all variables as equal. If they have used weightings, then ask what evidence the researchers have to justify their weights.

This chapter is the final one on standardisation. The next chapter, Chapter 7, introduces the idea of statistical correlations between two variables. And the following two chapters look in more detail at correlations between categorical variables and then numerical variables.

Part Three

Correlations

SEVEN

Introducing correlations

Chapter Overview	

This chapter will:

- Explain what a correlation or statistical association is, and how you can measure its strength, direction, and nature.
- Show that correlation and causation are not the same thing.
- Highlight the importance of spurious correlations that disappear when other variables are taken into account.

Much research focuses on the *correlation* between variables. A correlation is also known as an *association*. This and the following two chapters use these two terms interchangeably. It's important to be very clear about exactly what the terms mean:

A correlation or association occurs when your knowledge of the values of one variable allows you to predict more accurately the values of a second variable.

For example, if I ask you to predict whether a mystery person is called Jack or Jill, without more information you have a 50/50 chance of being right. But if you know that the person is a man, then you can use your knowledge about the correlation between Sex (one variable) and Name (a second variable) to make a prediction about the name of the mystery man that is almost certain to be correct. In other words, there is a statistical association between the variables Sex and Name.

The variable that chronologically comes first is termed the *independent variable*; not surprisingly, the other is the *dependent variable*. Parents wait until they know the sex of their child before they decide on a name. Thus, Sex is the independent variable, and Name is the dependent variable. A check on this is to ask which association makes more sense: name depending on sex; or sex depending on name? A child's name partly depends on its sex, but a child's sex does not depend on its name.

Many government departments now publish lists of the most popular names registered during the year (e.g. SSA (2009) in the USA, NSO (2009) in Britain, and NLA (2008) in Australia). A comparison of the top 10 most popular boys' and girls' names in Britain, the USA, and New South Wales in Australia shows a good deal of overlap: Joshua, William, Emily, Olivia, and Chloe were in all three top 10 lists, and Jack, James, Ethan, and Isabella appeared in two of the lists. When I looked at the top 100 boys' and girls' names in both the USA and Britain, no name appeared on both. In the previous year, there was only one name on both the boys' and girls' lists – *Jordan*, which was 45th in the US boys' list and 100th in the US girls' list.

To give a good description of a car you need to say something about its colour, model, and year. To give a good description of the distribution of a single variable you need measurements for the most typical value and the spread of the other values around it. To give a good description of the correlation or association between two variables, you need measurements for three characteristics: (i) strength, (ii) direction, and (iii) nature.

Consider, for example, the association between travelling speed and stopping distance. Generally, the faster you go, the longer it takes you to stop. This reflects the *direction* of the association.

But there isn't a steady increase in stopping distance with speed. For example, other things being equal, an increase in speed of 10 miles per hour (mph) from 20 to 30 results in an increase in stopping distance of about *11* metres (or *35* feet). An increase in speed of 10 mph from 40 to 50 results in an increase in stopping distance of about *17* metres (or *57* feet). And an increase of 10 mph in speed from 60 to 70 results in an increase in stopping distance of over *23* metres (or *75* feet) (*Highway Code* 2009: s.126). In other words, stopping distance increases at a faster rate as speed increases. These figures reflect the *nature* of the correlation.

But how typical are these stopping distances? Common sense suggests that stopping distance will vary depending on the driver, the car, and the road. For example, a drunk driver in an old car on a wet road is likely to take *much* longer to stop than a sober driver in a new car on a dry road. The accuracy with which you can predict stopping distance based solely on travelling speed reflects the *strength* of the correlation.

If the predictions are perfectly accurate, there is a *perfect correlation* between the variables. Such perfection is pretty much confined to the pages of statistics books. For a very simple illustration of a perfect association, imagine drinking a glass of water (or cola, milk, fruit juice, wine, or beer). The more you drink, the less there will be left in the glass. You can predict exactly the amount left in the glass once you know how much has been drunk. (I did say it was a very simple illustration!)

At the other extreme are those situations where knowledge of the values of one variable gives you absolutely no help when predicting the values of a second variable. Two variables that are absolutely unrelated are Sex and Eye colour. For example, if I ask you to predict whether a mystery person is a man or woman, you have a 50/50 chance of guessing correctly. If I then tell you that this person has blue eyes, you still have a 50/50 chance of guessing correctly. In other words, the accuracy of your prediction is no better than before. Thus, there is *zero correlation* between the variables Sex and Eye colour.

Correlation and causation

The basic aim of much research is to explain what causes things to happen. But so far I've talked about *correlation* rather than *causation*. The two terms are not interchangeable. A strong correlation between two variables does not necessarily indicate a cause and effect relationship. For example, in his classic text *Say It With Figures*, Hans Zeisel (1985: 143) refers to 'an old Chinese statistical joke' about how it is not a good idea to visit the doctor because statistics show that the more often people visit their doctor, the more likely they are to die! In other words, there is a correlation between the two variables:

Visits to doctor ➜ Death

This association is there, of course, because both variables are affected by a third – illness. You are more likely to visit a doctor if you are ill, and more likely to die if you are ill. Once you take this into account, the original correlation between visits to the doctor and death disappears:

Illness   Illness
↓   ↓
Visits to doctor → Death

Similarly, if you compare cities across the country, there is likely to be a strong correlation between the number of bookshops and the crime rate: the more bookshops, the higher the crime rate:

Bookshops ➜ Crime rate

However, this strong correlation does not mean that the number of bookshops has an effect on the crime rate (or that the crime rate has an effect on the number of bookshops). A correlation appears between bookshops and crime rate because both variables are affected by a third – city size:

City size   City size
↓   ↓
Bookshops → Crime rate

Generally, the larger the city, the more bookshops it contains; and the larger the city, the higher its crime rate. The correlation between bookshops and crime rate is a *spurious correlation* because it disappears when you take into account city size. It is for this reason that some researchers prefer the terms *explanatory variable* instead of independent variable and *response variable* instead of dependent variable.

In general, before you can say that there is a cause and effect relationship between two variables, three conditions must apply:

1 The cause variable must be present before the effect variable.
2 There must be a correlation between the two variables.
3 The correlation must not be spurious.

The major obstacle in this list for much social research is proving that a statistical association is not spurious.

Spurious correlations

Remember that a spurious correlation is one that disappears when you take other variables into account. The difficulty with this is that many other variables might be important. Some may be obvious, some not so obvious, and a few that possibly no one has thought of. The only way to be absolutely sure that a correlation is not spurious is to make sure that the *only* independent variable that could possibly have an effect on the dependent variable is the one that you are interested in. In other words, as Figure 7.1 shows, you must control all these extra variables (termed *extraneous variables*), manipulate the independent variable, and then measure the dependent variable to find out if a cause and effect relationship exists.

This level of control of the variables is possible only in experiments done under laboratory conditions. For example, Figure 7.2 shows the basic steps in a very simple psychology experiment designed to measure the effect of lack of sleep on memory.

The first step is to control the extraneous variables. You start by collecting together 100 individuals (usually called *subjects* in psychology) to take part in the experiment. You give each a number, and then divide them randomly into two groups of 50. In what Zeisel (1985: 131) terms 'the miracle of random selection',

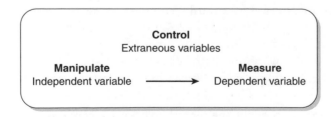

Figure 7.1   Ensuring associations are not spurious

GENERAL
PROCEDURE

SPECIFIC
EXAMPLE

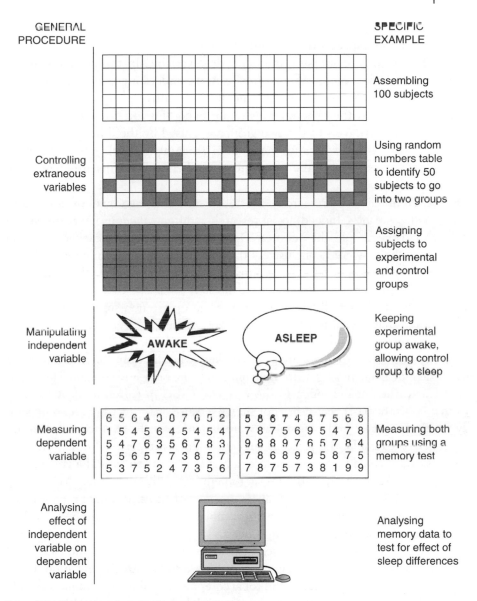

Assembling
100 subjects

Controlling
extraneous
variables

Using random
numbers table
to identify 50
subjects to go
into two groups

Assigning
subjects to
experimental
and control
groups

Manipulating
independent
variable

AWAKE

ASLEEP

Keeping
experimental
group awake,
allowing control
group to sleep

Measuring
dependent
variable

6	5	6	4	3	0	7	6	5	2
1	5	4	5	6	4	5	4	5	4
5	4	7	6	3	5	6	7	8	3
5	5	6	5	7	7	3	8	5	7
5	3	7	5	2	4	7	3	5	6

5	8	6	7	4	8	7	5	6	8
7	8	7	5	6	9	5	4	7	8
9	8	8	9	7	6	5	7	8	4
7	8	6	8	9	9	5	8	7	5
7	8	7	5	7	3	8	1	9	9

Measuring both
groups using a
memory test

Analysing
effect of
independent
variable on
dependent
variable

Analysing
memory data to
test for effect of
sleep differences

Figure 7.2   Basic steps in a simple experiment

you create two virtually identical groups. For example, the groups are likely to have the same average IQs, the same proportion of extroverts, the same overall level of attentiveness, the same proportion of blue-eyed people – and any other commonly occurring characteristic. In other words, random assignment of subjects to groups allows you to control extraneous variables.

The second step is to manipulate the independent variable. In this example, the independent variable is how much sleep the volunteers have. You manipulate the amount of sleep by keeping awake all night the 50 subjects in one group (the *experimental group*) while letting those in the other group (the *control group*) have a normal night's sleep. In the morning, the two previously identical groups now differ in just one respect – the amount of sleep.

The third step is to measure the dependent variable. In this experiment the dependent variable is memory, measured using a standard memory test. You compare the memory results of the experimental and control groups. If there are no problems in the way the experiment is set up (a big *If!*) you can say that any difference in memory levels of the two groups is caused by the differences in their sleeping patterns. This is because the random assignment of subjects to groups as far as possible ensures that the experimental and control groups are identical in all other respects.

However, much social research does not include this high level of direct control over the variables. Indeed, social researchers often *cannot* use experiments in their work. For example, the question 'Does smoking cause lung cancer in human beings?' can be answered conclusively through social research only by randomly assigning new born babies to two groups, and ensuring that, over the years, they have exactly the same environment and lifestyle – except that all those in one group are smokers, and all those in the other group are non-smokers. Only then can you say that any differences in the levels of lung cancer between the two groups is caused by smoking!

Simply comparing the percentage of smokers who die from lung cancer to the percentage of non-smokers who die from lung cancer is not enough. This argument leaves the research open to the very real criticism (often used by tobacco companies in the past) that it has not shown a cause and effect link. It could simply be that smokers and non-smokers are not necessarily identical in all other respects. For example, the smokers may have different personalities from non-smokers, and it could be this that causes a higher rate of cancer *and* a greater tendency to smoke. Consequently, the argument runs, although there is a strong correlation between smoking and cancer, the statistic is misleading because it is a spurious association. This is because both smoking and cancer could be caused by an extraneous variable, personality.

However, smokers cannot rejoice. *Genetic* research has proved the cause and effect link between smoking and lung cancer. A World Health Organization report notes that: 'In the 20th century, the tobacco epidemic killed 100 million people worldwide. During the 21st century, it could kill one billion' (WHO 2008: Preface).

If you cannot control all extraneous variables experimentally *before* you collect the data, you can control some of them statistically *after* you collect the data. Because the procedure involves testing the influence of specific extraneous variables, they are usually termed *test variables*. Unfortunately, no matter how many test variables you bring into the analysis, you can never be completely sure that the original correlation is not spurious (i.e. will not disappear once you introduce other test variables). The best you can do is say that the correlation is shown not to be spurious after taking into account the test variables used in the analysis.

The only time I have looked at *Lipids*, the journal of the American Oil Chemists' Society, was to read an article with the snappy title 'Increasing homicide rates and linoleic acid consumption among five western countries, 1961–2000' (Hibbeln et al. 2004). In fact, the article is full of fascinating international data showing a correlation between murder rates and the consumption of seed oils (mainly from takeaways, ready meals and snack foods). Both murder rates and seed oil consumption have increased rapidly over the last 40 years. However, aware that many other factors have also changed over this time, Hibbeln and his colleagues do not conclude that their data show a cause and effect association between the two variables. Instead, they call for more 'randomized controlled trials' (p. 1207) on both animals and humans.

This chapter provides some of the background for the following two chapters. These focus on how to measure the strength of a correlation between two variables and, more briefly, on the direction and nature of correlations.

EIGHT

Correlations between categories

> **Chapter Overview**
>
> This chapter will:
>
> - Recap on the meaning of a correlation or statistical association.
> - Show how a frequency table with *column percentages* gives a basic idea about the correlation between two categorical variables.
> - Show how a mosaic plot gives an immediate impression of the correlation between two categorical variables.
> - Go through the steps to calculate two basic correlation statistics, *percentage difference* and *lambda correlation coefficient*.

As you read this and the following chapter, it's very important that you never lose sight of exactly what *is* a correlation or statistical association. Remember the basic definition from the previous chapter. A correlation or statistical association occurs when your knowledge of the values of one variable (the *independent* variable) allows you to predict more accurately the values of a second variable (the *dependent* variable). The *strength* of the correlation is the level of accuracy of the prediction: the more accurate the prediction, the stronger the correlation between the two variables.

When dealing with numerical variables, you can also describe the *direction* and *nature* of the correlation – that is, *how* the values of the dependent variable change as the values of the independent variable change. However, categorical variables are, by definition, measured by placing individuals into categories, and most of the time there is no in-built order to the categories. For example, the US Census asks people born in the USA for their state of birth. These 'categories' (e.g. Alabama, Wyoming) have no inherent order – you can't say that in terms of birthplace Wyoming is 'more' or 'less' than Alabama. Certainly, Wyoming is larger in land area and smaller in population than Alabama. But the variables Land area and Population are different from Birthplace. As a result, the direction and nature of an association do not apply to categorical variables.

When the measurement process involves simply placing units of analysis into a handful of categories, the options you have for data analysis are more limited than when you're dealing with numerical variables. This chapter starts by showing how you can describe correlations or associations between categorical variables using frequency tables and bar graphs. It then outlines various ways to measure these associations with a number of easily calculated statistics.

Frequency tables

Table 8.1 contains information about one categorical variable, Exam result, categorised in the simplest way possible – into only two categories, Pass and Fail. (If there was only one possible category, then it wouldn't be a *variable* because, by definition, the values of a variable must be able to vary.) Table 8.1 is called a *frequency table* because it shows the frequency with which students passed and failed the exam: 997 students passed and 323 failed.

Table 8.2 is based on the same 1320 students as Table 8.1, but shows information about *two* variables: (i) Exam result and (ii) Sex. Table 8.2 is a two-by-two (2 × 2) *cross-tabulation* because it shows data in two rows and two columns. Sex is the independent variable and Exam result is the dependent variable. The general convention is to list the independent variable categories (Men and Women) in the columns, and the dependent variable categories (Pass and Fail) in the rows.

A two-by-two cross-tabulation has data in four boxes (or *cells*). In Table 8.2, the cells show: (i) how many men pass; (ii) how many men fail; (iii) how many women pass; and (iv) how many women fail. A table can also include row and column totals (called *marginals*). Table 8.2 shows only column totals to help draw your attention to the two columns, which show the two categories of the independent variable. Finally, of course, a table needs clear headings for the columns and rows to identify: (i) the variables (i.e. Sex, Exam result) and (ii) the categories of each variable (i.e. Men and Women, Pass and Fail).

As it stands, the frequency values in Table 8.2 are too large for most people to handle comfortably. One way to make life easier is to standardise the table using

Table 8.1 Frequency table showing one variable

Exam result	Frequency
Pass	997
Fail	323
Total	**1320**

Source: Hypothetical

Table 8.2 Frequency table showing two variables

	Sex	
Exam result	Men	Women
Pass	584	413
Fail	146	177
Total	**730**	**590**

column percentages. Basically, you find out: (i) what percentage of men passed, and what percentage of men failed; and (ii) what percentage of women passed, and what percentage of women failed. The calculations are based on the standard percentage equation:

$$\text{Cell percentage} = \frac{\text{Cell frequency}}{\text{Column total frequency}} \times 100$$

For example, 584 men passed the exam from a total of 730 men. Thus, the percentage of men who passed is as follows:

$$\text{Men/Pass cell \%} = \frac{584}{730} \times 100 = 0.8 \times 100 = 80$$

Table 8.3 shows this and the other column percentage values. Notice that the table also shows in brackets at the bottom of each column the actual number of men and women – 730 men and 590 women ('*N*' stands for Number). This is so that none of the original information is lost in the table. It also helps readers avoid making generalisations from percentage tables based on very small frequencies. For example, the finding that 100% of men eat only lean meat and 100% of women eat only fatty meat becomes somewhat less significant when you know that the figures come from a survey of Jack Spratt and his wife!

Table 8.3 Column percentages

Exam result	Men	Women
	Sex	
Pass	80	70
Fail	20	30
Total	**100**	**100**
	(*N* = 730)	(*N* = 590)

BEHIND THE STATS

'Jack Spratt could eat no fat/His wife could eat no lean./And so between them both, you see/They licked the platter clean.' Like many nursery rhymes, this one goes back several hundred years. 'Jack' is the British King Charles I (1600–49). The 'platter' is England, which he 'licked clean' (i.e. taxed heavily). The rhyme may have started to allow people to criticise the king without them ending up in prison, or worse. The story does not have a happy ending for Charles. After losing two civil wars, he was executed in 1649. Oliver Cromwell then set up a republican government (see Roberts 2004). Jack Spratt's unnamed wife, Queen Henrietta Maria, fled to France, later returning when the monarchy was restored under her son, Charles II. The US state of Maryland is named after her.

What does Table 8.3 say about the strength of the correlation between the two variables, Exam result and Sex? A useful approach is to compare the table you have to what it would look like in two extreme situations: (i) if there is a *perfect* correlation between the two variables; and (ii) if there is *zero* correlation between the two variables. Table 8.4 shows these.

Table 8.4   Perfect and zero correlations

8.4(a): Perfect correlation			8.4(b): Zero correlation		
	Sex			Sex	
Exam	Men	Women	Exam	Men	Women
Pass	100	0	Pass	100	100
Fail	0	100	Fail	0	0
Total	**100**	**100**	**Total**	**100**	**100**

Table 8.4(a) shows a perfect correlation between the two variables, Exam result and Sex. For example, once you know that a student is a man, you can predict with perfect accuracy that he passed the exam. This is because *all* men passed the exam. Similarly, once you know that a student is a woman, you can predict with perfect accuracy that she failed the exam because *all* women failed. (The example is completely fictional!) More generally, in a perfect correlation, once you know the independent variable category for any individual, you can predict with perfect accuracy the associated dependent variable category of that individual.

Table 8.4(b) shows a zero correlation between Exam result and Sex. *All* students, both male and female, passed the exam, and so without knowing the sex of an individual, you can predict his of her exam result (Pass) and be right every time. Clearly, you can't improve on this level of accuracy by knowing the sex of each student. Now, a correlation occurs only when your knowledge of the values of the independent variable allows you to predict the values of the dependent variable *more accurately*. Here, knowledge of whether the students are men or women results in zero improvement in the accuracy of the prediction about whether the students have passed or failed. Table 8.4(b) therefore shows a zero correlation.

Mosaic plots

A two-by-two cross-tabulation is the most basic way to say something about the strength of the correlation between two categorical variables. Another technique is to draw a special type of bar graph called a *mosaic plot*. It's simply a divided bar graph that, as Figure 8.1 shows, closely matches the format of a frequency table.

The bars of the mosaic plot (just like the columns of the table) show the categories of the independent variable (i.e. Men and Women). Each bar is divided by the categories of the dependent variable (i.e. Pass and Fail). To simplify a direct visual comparison, the two divided bars are always side by side with no gap

Exam	Men	Women
Pass	80	70
Fail	20	30
Total	**100**	**100**

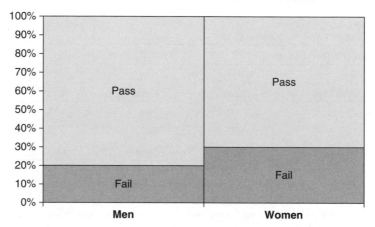

Figure 8.1   Mosaic plot

between them. The divided bars also have the same overall height. This means that before graphing the data, you always standardise the original frequencies to column percentages. This converts each column total to 100%. You read the mosaic plot in exactly the same way as the frequency table. The bigger the difference between the two divided bars, the stronger the correlation between the variables. Figure 8.2 allows you to compare mosaic plots showing the full range of correlation from zero to perfect.

The largest difference between the 'divided' bars appears in Figure 8.2(a). The bars do not look divided because each column is a single colour; the other colour is missing because one category has zero frequency (i.e. Men: Fail = 0; Women: Pass = 0). This occurs only when there is a perfect correlation between the variables. Figure 8.2(b) shows a big difference in the appearance of the two divided bars, indicating a strong association between Sex and the Exam II results. Figure 8.2(c) shows a small difference between the divided bars, indicating a weak association between Sex and the Exam III results. And Figure 8.2(d) shows zero difference between the divided bars, indicating that there is zero correlation between Sex and the Exam IV results.

On their own, tables and graphs give a useful first impression of the association between two variables, but they provide a rather hazy picture. Often, it is useful to quantify the strength of a correlation between two variables with a single statistic. The following sections look at two basic techniques: (i) the percentage difference; and (ii) the slightly more sophisticated lambda correlation coefficient.

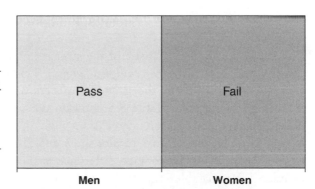

8.2A: Perfect

Exam I	Men	Women
Pass	100	0
Fail	0	100
Total	**100**	**100**

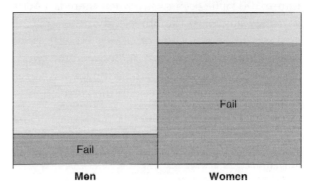

8.2B: Strong

Exam II	Men	Women
Pass	90	10
Fail	10	90
Total	**100**	**100**

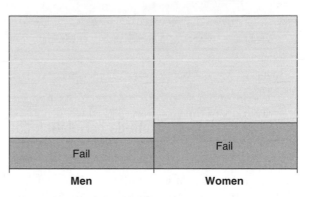

8.2C: Weak

Exam III	Men	Women
Pass	80	70
Fail	20	30
Total	**100**	**100**

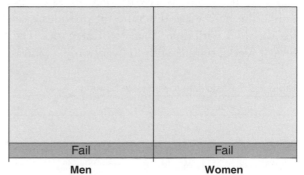

8.2D: Zero

Exam IV	Men	Women
Pass	90	90
Fail	10	10
Total	**100**	**100**

Figure 8.2   Mosaic plots showing perfect to zero correlations

Percentage differences

The simplest summary statistic of the strength of a correlation between two categorical variables is the *percentage difference*. This is the difference between the two percentage values on the same row of a conventional 2 × 2 table standardised to column percentages. Table 8.5 shows again some earlier data, but this time including percentage difference values.

For example, the Exam I results show that 100% of men passed and 0% of women passed. The percentage difference is therefore 100, the maximum percentage difference value (i.e. 100–0, or 0–100 ignoring the minus sign). This maximum 100 value occurs only when there is a perfect correlation between the two variables shown. At the other end of the range, the Exam IV results show a percentage difference value of 0 (e.g. 90–90). A percentage difference value of 0 shows there is zero correlation between the two variables. The closer the percentage difference gets to 100, the stronger the correlation; the closer the percentage difference gets to 0, the weaker the correlation.

Table 8.5   Percentage differences

	Exam I		Exam II		Exam III		Exam IV	
Exam result	M	W	M	W	M	W	M	W
Pass	100	0	90	10	80	70	90	90
Fail	0	100	10	90	20	30	10	10
Percentage difference	100		80		10		0	
Strength of association	Perfect		Strong		Weak		Zero	

Lambda correlation coefficient

Another measure of association for categorical data is the *lambda* correlation coefficient (not to be confused with the lambada!). Lambda is the letter 'L' in the Greek alphabet. It's almost as easy to calculate as the percentage difference statistic and, unlike the percentage difference, it provides a single-figure correlation coefficient for variables with more than two categories. The following few paragraphs show how it works, starting with the very simple (and very artificial) data in Table 8.6.

Table 8.6   Basic data to illustrate lambda

8.6(a): Cards: type		8.6(b): Cards: type by colour			
			Card colour		
Card type	Total	Card type	Red	Black	Total
Number	15	Number	13	2	15
Face	10	Face	1	9	10
Total	**25**	**Total**	**14**	**11**	**25**

You have a pile of 25 playing cards lying face down on the table in front of you. As Table 8.6(a) shows, overall there are 15 *number* cards (e.g. 5, 6, 7) and 10 *face* cards (i.e. Jack, Queen, King). I show you Table 8.6(a), and then ask you to guess what type, number, or face each card will be. After a moment's thought, you guess 'number card' each time, because you have 15 chances of being right, and only 10 chances of being wrong.

What if I now separate the 25 cards into two piles, one with the 14 red cards and the other with the 11 black cards? I show you Table 8.6(b), and then ask you to guess what type, number or face, each black card and each red card will be. Table 8.6(b) shows that in the red pile there are 13 number cards and 1 face card. You therefore guess that each of the red cards is a number card. You are right 13 times and wrong just once. When guessing cards in the black pile, you know from Table 8.6(b) that there are 9 face cards and 2 number cards. You therefore predict that each of the black cards is a face card. You are right 9 times and wrong 2 times.

BEHIND THE STATS

One legend is that cards originated in the Chinese imperial palace. For some 2000 years, the emperor's 'mistresses of the bed' included (apart from the empress) 3 consorts, 9 spouses, 27 concubines, and 81 assistant concubines. The legend is that 'playing cards were conceived by an inmate of the Chinese imperial harem as a pastime for relieving perpetual boredom' (Tilley 1973: 7).

Statisticians focus on the number of *errors* in the guesses or predictions. Initially, without information about card colour, you made 10 errors (i.e. the 10 face cards you predicted to be number cards). This is the *original error*. Later, with information about card colour, you made a total of 3 errors (1 with red cards and 2 with black cards). This is the *remaining error* because it's the prediction error that remains even when you have information about the independent variable (Colour).

The lambda statistic uses the difference between original error and remaining error. Like many correlation coefficients, lambda is a *proportional reduction in error* statistic because it measures how much the prediction error has reduced as a proportion of what it was originally:

$$\begin{matrix} \text{Lambda correlation} \\ \text{coefficient} \end{matrix} = \begin{matrix} \text{Proportional} \\ \text{reduction in error} \end{matrix} = \frac{\text{Original error} - \text{Remaining error}}{\text{Original error}}$$

In the card example, when you make the predictions *without* knowledge of card colour, there are 10 original errors. When you make the predictions *with* knowledge of card colour, there are 3 remaining errors. The equation below shows the calculation for lambda, the proportional reduction in error:

$$\text{Lambda correlation coefficient} = \frac{\text{Original error} - \text{Remaining error}}{\text{Original error}} = \frac{10 - 3}{10} = \frac{7}{10} = 0.70$$

A lambda correlation coefficient of 0.70 shows that when predicting whether cards will be number cards or face cards, your knowledge of the colour of each card leads to a proportional reduction in error of 0.70. In other words, there is a percentage reduction in error of 70% (i.e. the number of original errors went down by 70%). The interpretation of the lambda coefficient in this way is a feature common to all the coefficients based on the idea of a proportional reduction in error.

If there's a zero correlation between variables, the lambda coefficient is 0. This is to be expected as in a zero correlation knowledge of the values of the independent variable results in a zero improvement in the accuracy of the predictions about the values of the dependent variable. At the other end of the range, if there's a perfect correlation between variables, the lambda coefficient is 1. In other words, the original errors have been reduced by 100% – so that now there aren't any. Again this is to be expected, as a perfect correlation means that knowledge of the values of the independent variable results in perfectly accurate predictions about the values of the dependent variable.

Now that you have got the idea behind lambda, it's worth showing how it works with a more real-life example. The data in Table 8.7 are a slightly simplified version of results from a UK public opinion poll about attitudes to nuclear power stations.

Table 8.7   Attitudes to nuclear power, by sex, UK

Attitude	Sex		Total
	Men	Women	
Support	450	250	700
Neutral	350	400	750
Oppose	200	350	550
Total	**1000**	**1000**	**2000**

Source: Data simplified from Ipsos MORI 2007

Clearly, there's a difference in the attitudes of men and women to nuclear power – men are more supportive than women. In other words, the table shows that there is *some* association between the variables, Attitude and Sex. The lambda coefficient measures the strength of this association. The Total column of Table 8.7 shows that the most common answer is 'Neutral', with 750 of 2000 respondents giving this response. Thus, when you don't know the sex of each respondent, your best guess about how all 2000 people answered the question is 'Neutral'. Using this answer, you are right 750 times and wrong 1250 times (700 + 550). Thus, 1250 is the original error.

When you do know each respondent's sex, you would choose 'Support' for all 1000 men, and you'd be right 450 times and wrong 550 times (350 + 200). For women, you'd say 'Neutral', and be right 400 times and wrong 600 times (250 + 350). Overall, the remaining error is 1150 (550 + 600). Put these error values into the lambda formula:

$$\text{Lambda} = \frac{\text{Original error} - \text{Remaining error}}{\text{Original error}} = \frac{1250 - 1150}{1250} = \frac{100}{1250} = 0.08$$

The lambda coefficient of 0.08 shows that when predicting attitudes to nuclear power, your knowledge of the sex of the respondents leads to a proportional reduction in error of 0.08, or a percentage reduction in error of 8%.

On a range of 0 to 1 (or 0% to 100%), a lambda value of 0.08 (8%) shows a weak correlation between the variables Attitude and Sex. However, Sex is only one of a number of possibly influential variables on people's attitudes to nuclear power. Looked at in this light, the 8% reduction in error is likely to lead researchers to look more closely at this correlation.

Table 8.7 shows that men are more in favour of nuclear power than are women: 45% of men (450 of 1000) support it compared to only 25% of women. Why does this difference occur? Table 8.7 doesn't tell you. You need more information from further research. For example, is the difference in attitude because men focus more on economic issues and women (particularly mothers) more on family issues? Freudenburg and Davidson (2007: 215) note that 'the underlying reasons have never been well-clarified'. Generally, explaining something is often much more difficult than describing it.

Make sure that you never put data into a formula in a mindless fashion. For example, lambda is limited in the patterns of data it can handle. The focus on the largest frequencies in each column means that if the cells with the largest frequencies lie on the same row of the table, then lambda is *always* zero. This happens even when there clearly is a correlation between the variables. For example, Table 8.8 shows some results from another survey on attitudes to nuclear power, this time across the European Union.

The differences in attitudes between men and women are similar to the British survey, and you might expect a similar lambda value. But Table 8.8 shows that the largest value in the Men column (6600) lies on the same row as the largest value in the Women column (9050). Remember that whenever this occurs, the lambda value is *always* zero. In other words, in these situations, the lambda calculation is worthless.

So, if lambda is inappropriate, how can you measure the strength of the correlation between these variables? The simplest option is to draw a mosaic plot. Regardless of its complexity, you always read a mosaic plot in the same way: the greater the difference between the bars, the stronger the correlation between the variables. Figure 8.3 shows the mosaic plot of the column percentages in Table 8.8.

Table 8.8   Inappropriate data for lambda: attitudes to nuclear power, by sex, European Union

	Sex				
	Men		Women		
Attitude	N	%	N	%	Total
Support	4850	39	2750	21	7600
Neutral	950	8	1550	12	2500
Oppose	6600	53	9050	68	15650
Total	**12,400**	**100**	**13,350**	**100**	**25,750**

Source: Data based on Gallup 2007: Table 9b

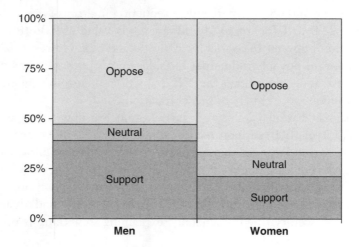

Figure 8.3   Attitudes to nuclear power, by sex, European Union
Source: Data based on Gallup 2007: Table 9b

It shows at a glance the quite large difference in the attitudes of men and women to nuclear power and thus the quite strong correlation between the variables.

If you want to use percentage differences to measure the strength of the association between these variables, then you need to reduce the number of Attitude categories to two, so that you end up with a 2 × 2 table. Statistically, it is quite easy to combine categories. But which combination is best? For example:

- You can combine Oppose and Neutral into a single 'Not support' category. You thus end up with two attitude categories: (i) Not support and (ii) Support.
- You can combine Support and Neutral into a single 'Not oppose' category. You thus end up with two attitude categories: (i) Not oppose and (ii) Oppose.
- You can leave out the Neutral respondents altogether, and have just the original Support and Oppose groups.

The first two of these three options are questionable. The Not support v Support option is most likely to be used by opponents of nuclear power because it adds the Neutral group to the Oppose group. The Not oppose v Oppose option is most likely to be used by supporters of nuclear power because it adds the Neutral group to the Support group.

As Table 8.9 shows, the best option is to leave out the Neutral category and compare just the original Support and Oppose groups. Note that with this final option you recalculate the column percentages using only the frequencies of the two remaining groups. You don't take the original column percentages from Table 8.8 because they are based on all three Attitude categories. Table 8.9 shows that there's a percentage difference value of 19, showing a moderately strong association between the variables Sex and Attitude to nuclear power. Once again, women are more opposed than men (though a majority of *both* sexes are against nuclear power).

Table 8.9   Simplifying data into a 2 × 2 table: attitudes to nuclear power, by sex, European Union

Attitude	Sex	
	Men	Women
Support	42	23
Oppose	58	77
% difference	**19**	

This chapter is about how to measure correlations between two categorical variables. The next chapter, Chapter 9, also looks at correlations, but focuses on numerical variables.

NINE

Correlations between numbers

Chapter Overview

This chapter will:

- Recap on the meaning of *correlation* or *statistical association*.
- Illustrate how a *scattergraph* shows the strength and direction of a correlation between two numerical variables.
- Show how to position a *best-fit line* onto a scattergraph.
- Show how to calculate a *coefficient of determination* to measure the strength of the association between two numerical variables.
- Show how to calculate an *eta-squared correlation coefficient* to measure the strength of the association between one numerical variable and one categorical variable.

Remember that a correlation (or association) occurs when your knowledge of the values of the independent variable allows you to predict more accurately the values of the dependent variable. The strength of the association is the level of accuracy of the prediction: the more accurate the prediction, the stronger the correlation between the two variables.

Chapter 8 showed how to describe the strength of a correlation between categorical variables. This chapter shows how to describe the strength of a correlation between two numerical variables. In a numerical variable, each individual (or unit of analysis) is measured with a number. This means that there are many more unique values than occur with categorical variables, where you place the units of analysis into only a handful of categories. In addition, you can manipulate numbers in ways that are impossible with named categories. Because numerical data are not as simple as categorical data, the measures of correlations are also not as simple. However, the underlying ideas driving the statistical analysis are the same as outlined in Chapter 7.

As with categorical variables, you can use tables, graphs, and statistics to measure correlations between numerical variables. However, when you convert numerical data to tables you inevitably lose much of the original information. Thus, with numerical data it's better to use graphs and statistics because they use all the original information. This chapter focuses on one type of graph, the *scattergraph*, and two correlation coefficients, the *coefficient of determination* and the *eta-squared coefficient*. Much of the chapter is based on the hypothetical data in Table 9.1. It shows how 25 respondents scored on a survey designed to look at the relationship between two variables, happiness and social integration.

Table 9.1   Happiness and Integration index values

Respondent ID	Integration index	Happiness index	Respondent ID	Integration index	Happiness index
A	100	124	N	190	150
B	100	125	O	200	150
C	110	125	P	200	155
D	120	130	Q	200	170
E	120	135	R	200	160
F	140	125	S	210	150
G	150	115	T	210	140
H	150	145	U	220	172
I	160	145	V	220	175
J	170	142	W	250	180
K	170	175	X	270	205
L	180	149	Y	300	215
M	190	165			

Source: Hypothetical

Happiness is a complex concept. Seligman et al. (2005: 276) identify three 'constituents': pleasure, engagement, and meaning. In the hypothetical data used here, happiness is measured by a Happiness index, which ranges between 0 and 250.

▬▬▬▬▬▬▬▬▬▬   BEHIND THE STATS   ▬▬▬▬▬▬▬▬▬▬

Happiness is now a major focus of research. In the first issue of the *Journal of Happiness Studies*, the editor justifies the new journal, saying 'Currently we know more about headaches than about happiness' (Veenhoven 2000: viii). A 'World Poll' by Gallup lists Finland as the world's happiest country. Gallup's unsurprising overall finding is that 'In all the rich places ... most people say they are happy. In all the poor ones (mainly Africa), people say they are not' (*The Economist*, 14 July 2007: 63). Sydney is home to the 'Happiness Institute', headed by the self-styled 'Dr Happy' (aka Dr Timothy Sharp, a clinical psychologist).

Social integration refers to the quantity and intensity of people's social networks through membership of various groups and participation in informal activities with family, friends, and others. It also includes the level of trust that people have in various social institutions, such as the police and courts. In the hypothetical data used here, social integration is measured using an Integration index, ranging from 0 to 300. Helliwell (2006: C38) sums up the literature about the association between happiness and social integration, saying 'The more we get together the happier we'll be.'

Scattergraphs and best-fit lines

The usual way to create a visual impression of the strength of a correlation between two numerical variables is with a *scattergraph* (also called a *scattergram* or *scatterplot*). Figure 9.1 shows a scattergraph of the data in Table 9.1.

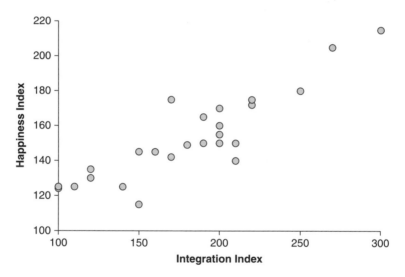

Figure 9.1   Happiness and Integration indexes

The two edges or lines on the graph are *axes* (the singular is *axis*). The horizontal axis shows the independent variable, and the vertical axis shows the dependent variable. Each point on the scattergraph represents one of the 25 respondents listed in Table 9.1. For example, the top right-hand point shows Respondent Y, who has an Integration score of 300 and a Happiness score of 215. To find the correct position for this person on the scattergraph, you have to go along the horizontal axis to the 300 mark and then up the vertical axis to 215. The symbol for Respondent Y is where these two (imaginary) lines meet.

How does the scattergraph help you to say something about the strength of the correlation between the two variables? Remember that perfect and zero correlations are the two extremes. If you know which pattern of points shows a perfect correlation, and which pattern shows a zero correlation, you can compare any scattergraph to these to get an indication of the strength of the correlation between the two variables.

With a perfect correlation, you can predict with absolute accuracy the values of the dependent variable from the values of the independent variable. What strikes you about the following data?

Independent variable	1	2	3	4	5	6	7	8	9	10
Dependent variable	2	4	6	8	10	12	14	16	18	20

The values of the dependent variable are always double those of the independent variable. Thus, once you know a particular value for the independent variable, you can work out with absolute accuracy the corresponding dependent value. In other words, the two variables have a perfect association

What about the other end of the range – where there is zero correlation between two variables? What strikes you about the data below?

Independent variable	0	0	0	0	1	1	1	1	2	2	2	2	3	3	3	3
Dependent variable	0	1	2	3	0	1	2	3	0	1	2	3	0	1	2	3

Knowledge of the values of the independent variable gives you no help when predicting the values of the dependent variable because each independent value is linked with the whole range of dependent values. For example, the zeros in the independent variable row are linked with a 0, 1, 2, and 3 in the dependent variable row. The scattergraphs in Figure 9.2 show these perfect and zero correlations.

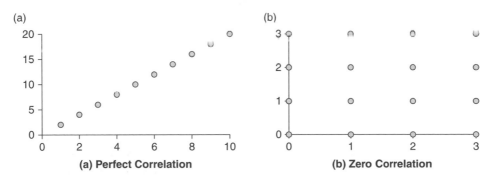

Figure 9.2   Perfect and zero correlations

Figure 9.2(a) shows a perfect correlation. Notice that the points lie in a completely straight line. For the moment, we can say that a perfect correlation has a pattern of points that can be joined together perfectly by a sloping straight line. The line will not always cross the vertical axis at the same point, nor will it always be at the same angle from the horizontal axis. But the straight line always joins all the points. Figure 9.2(b) shows a zero correlation. Notice that the points are as widely scattered as they can be across the graph. Any scattergraph showing a zero correlation will have the same widely scattered pattern of points.

The Happiness–Integration scattergraph in Figure 9.1 looks more like the perfect correlation graph than the zero correlation graph. You can't join all the points by the one straight line, but as Figure 9.3 shows, a straight line that goes through the middle of the points is not far from any of them. Overall, the closer the points are to the line, the better the line summarises the scatter of points. This means that, using only the summary line, you can make a fairly accurate prediction of the value of the dependent variable (Happiness) associated with a given value of the independent variable (Integration). The line that best fits the scatter of points is the *best-fit line*.

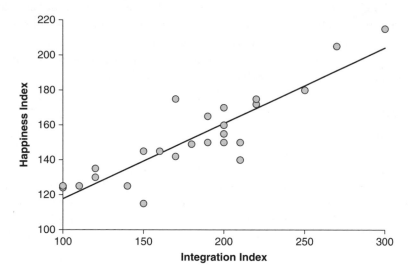

Figure 9.3   Scattergraph with best-fit line

There are a number of ways to draw a best-fit line through a scatter of points on a scattergraph. The easiest way is to do it by eye. When the points form a straight line (i.e. when there is a perfect correlation), everyone's summary line is in the same place. However, the more scattered the points are on the graph (i.e. the weaker the correlation), the more likely it is that there will be disagreement about exactly where the line should go. In contrast, people always draw the best-fit line in exactly the same place when they use the statistical technique described below.

The best-fit line is a bit like the mean. Just as the mean summarises the centre of the distribution of the values of one variable, the best-fit line summarises the centre of the scatter of points showing the association between the two variables. For historical reasons, a best-fit line is usually called a *regression line*.

BEHIND THE STATS

Frances Galton (1822–1911), a cousin of Charles Darwin, had many interests, including exploration, heredity, meteorology, fingerprinting, word association – and statistics. In 1885, he wrote a paper comparing the heights of parents and their children. Couples who were taller than the mean tended to have children who were shorter than they were. In contrast, couples who were shorter than the mean tended to have children who were taller than they were. Galton used the term *regression* to describe how heights tend to move back (or *regress*) to the mean. This research led him in the 1870s to draw the first regression line on a scattergraph (Tankard 1984: Ch3).

How exactly do you work out where to draw the regression line on a scatter-graph? I'll use the following small data set to show the basic thinking behind the statistics:

Independent variable values	Dependent variable values
1	2
2	1
4	3
5	4

You might expect (and you'd be right) that the mean of the dependent variable is associated with the mean of the independent variable. Thus, if asked what value of the dependent variable is most likely to be associated with the mean of the independent variable, your best bet is to say 'the mean of the dependent variable'. In this small data set, the mean of the independent variable is 3.0 and the mean of the dependent variable is 2.5. You can use these two values to mark a point on the graph (the *mean point*) that the regression line passes through:

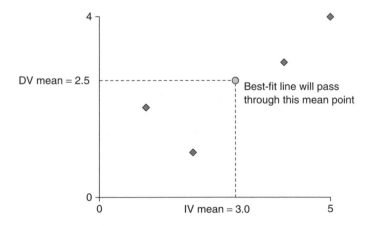

You now need to know the *slope* of the line as it passes through this mean point:

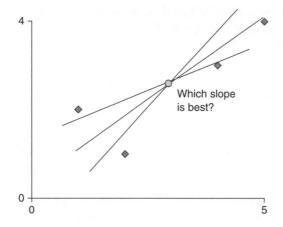

Calculating the slope of the regression line is less straightforward. Statisticians use the equation:

$$\text{Slope} = \frac{\text{Covariance of independent variable and dependent variable}}{\text{Variance of independent variable}}$$

The term on the bottom line, *variance*, was first mentioned in Chapter 2. Table 9.2(a) shows that in this small data set, the variance is 2.5. The term on the top line, *Covariance* is a new term. It measures the average amount by which deviations from the mean of the dependent variable are associated with deviations from the mean of the independent variable. If the two variables do not co-vary at all (i.e. if there is zero correlation between them) then the covariance is 0. There is no set maximum value as it depends on the size of the original values. Table 9.2(b) shows that in this small data set the covariance is 1.5. Table 9.2(c) shows that, using these variance and covariance values, the slope of the regression line is +0.60.

Table 9.2　Slope of regression line

9.2a: Variance of IV			
Value	Mean	Difference	Squared difference
1	3	−2	−2 × −2 = 4
2	3	−1	−1 × −1 = 1
4	3	+1	+1 × +1 = 1
5	3	+2	+2 × +2 = 4
			Sum of squares = 10

Variance = Sum of squares ÷ Number of values = 10 ÷ 4 = **2.5**

9.2(b): Covariance of IV and DV

IV values	IV mean	IV difference	DV values	DV mean	DV difference	IV difference × DV difference
1	3	−2	2	2.5	−0.5	−2 × −0.5 = 1.0
2	3	−1	1	2.5	−1.5	−1 × −1.5 = 1.5
4	3	+1	3	2.5	+0.5	+1 × +0.5 = 0.5
5	3	+2	4	2.5	+1.5	+2 × +1.5 = 3.0
						Sum of products = 6.0

Covariance = Sum of products ÷ Number of pairs of values = 6.0 ÷ 4 = **+1.5**

9.2(c). Slope

$$\textbf{Slope} = \frac{\text{Covariance of independent variable and dependent variable}}{\text{Variance of independent variable}} = \frac{1.5}{2.5} = \textbf{+0.60}$$

A slope value of +0.6 means that for every increase of 1 in the independent variable, there is an increase of 0.6 in the dependent variable. Table 9.3 shows how it works. Start in the middle at the row showing the two means. Reading up the table, you'll see that as the independent variable values increase by 1, the dependent variable values increase by 0.6. Similarly, reading down the table, as the independent variable values decrease by 1, the dependent variable values decrease by 0.6. Notice that when the independent variable value is 0, the dependent variable value is 0.7. The 0.7 value is known as the *intercept* because it is where the regression line intercepts (i.e. cuts through) the vertical axis when the horizontal axis starts at 0.

Table 9.3   Slope and intercept values

IV value Values change by 1		DV value prediction Values change by 0.6
6.0	↔	4.3
5.0	↔	3.7
4.0	↔	3.1
Mean = 3.0	↔	2.5 = Mean
2.0	↔	1.9
1.0	↔	1.3
0.0	↔	**0.7 = Intercept**

You now have two very useful statistical measures of the regression line:

- *Intercept* Where the regression line cuts through the vertical axis.
- *Slope* The slope of the regression line as it goes across the graph.

You use the slope and the intercept values in a *regression equation* to describe the position of the regression line. It has the following general form:

Predicted dependent variable value = Intercept + (Slope × Independent variable value)

With an intercept value of 0.7 and a slope value of 0.6, the regression equation for the small data set is:

Predicted DV value = 0.7 + (0.6 × Chosen IV value)

So, for example, if you chose 3 as the independent variable value, your prediction of the associated dependent variable value is:

Predicted DV value = 0.7 + (0.6 × 3) = 0.7 + 1.8 = 2.5

This result confirms the earlier comment that the mean of the dependent variable (2.5) is associated with the mean of the independent variable (3.0). Figure 9.4 summarises the use of the intercept and slope values when describing a regression line.

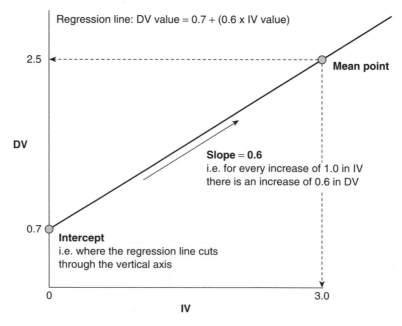

Figure 9.4   Intercept and slope.

So far, the chapter has used very simple data to illustrate where to position a regression line on a scattergraph. However, exactly the same series of steps applies to a larger data set, such as that about happiness and social integration shown in Table 9.1. The table below shows the steps needed to find the slope and intercept values:

Step	Statistic	Values
1	Mean of Integration	181.2
2	Mean of Happiness	152.9
3	Variance of Integration	2522.6
4	Covariance of Integration and Happiness	1090.2
5	Slope	0.43
6	Intercept	74.6

With an intercept value of 74.6 and a slope value of 0.43, the regression equation is as follows:

Predicted Happiness value = 74.6 + (0.43 × Chosen Integration value)

Thus, if you want to include a regression line in Figure 9.1, where the Integration axis starts at 100 and ends at 300, you simply put these values into the regression equation:

Predicted Happiness value for an Integration value of 100 = 74.6 + (0.43 × 100) = 118

Predicted Happiness value for an Integration value of 300 = 74.6 + (0.43 × 300) = 204

You then use these Integration/Happiness co-ordinates (100/118 and 300/204) to give you two points to join up with the regression line.

Coefficient of determination

This section explains the thinking behind measuring the strength of a correlation between two numerical variables using a single-figure summary statistic called the *coefficient of determination*. Recall that a correlation or association exists when your knowledge of the values of the independent variable allows you to predict more accurately the values of the dependent variable. The coefficient of determination is a proportional reduction in error measure, which once again you calculate as follows:

$$\text{Coefficient of determination} = \frac{\text{Original error} - \text{Remaining error}}{\text{Original error}}$$

The original error is the error made when you predict the values of the dependent variable *without* knowledge of the values of the independent variable. The remaining error is what remains when you predict the values of the dependent variable *with* knowledge of the values of the independent variable. The very simple data set from the previous section shows the basic idea:

Independent variable values	Dependent variable values
1	2
2	1
4	3
5	4

First, you measure the original error – the error that you make when you predict values of the dependent variable *without* knowledge of the values of the independent variable. Overall, predictions about dependent variable values will be most accurate when you choose a value that is typical of the data set. The *mean* is the obvious choice. In this example, the mean of the dependent variable is 2.5. Thus, when asked to guess an dependent variable value, you always say '2.5'. As Table 9.4 shows, on two occasions your prediction is too low, and on two occasions your prediction is too high. You use the variance of these prediction errors as a single-figure measure of the original error. In this example, the variance of the prediction errors is 1.25, and thus the original error is 1.25.

Table 9.4   Coefficient of determination – original error

Observed DV values	Predicted DV values (DV mean)	Differences between observed and predicted DV values	Squared differences between observed and predicted DV values
2	2.5	2 – 2.5 = –0.5	(–0.5) × (–0.5) = 0.25
1	2.5	1 – 2.5 = –1.5	(–1.5) × (–1.5) = 2.25
3	2.5	3 – 2.5 = +0.5	(+0.5) × (+0.5) = 0.25
4	2.5	4 – 2.5 = +1.5	(+1.5) × (+1.5) = 2.25
			Sum of squares = 5.00

$$\text{Variance} = \frac{\text{Sum of squares}}{\text{Number of values}} = \frac{5.00}{4} = 1.25 = \text{Original error}$$

You now measure the remaining error – the error that remains when you predict values of the dependent variable *with* knowledge of the values of the independent variable. You can make precise predictions using the regression equation. As the section on scattergraphs shows, the regression equation for this very simple data set is:

Predicted Dependent Variable value = 0.7 + (0.6 × Chosen Independent Variable value)

For example, if the chosen independent variable value is 4.0, you use the above regression equation to find the most likely dependent variable value as follows:

Predicted DV value when IV value is 4.0 = 0.7 + (0.6 × 4.0) = 3.1

Thus, when the independent variable (IV) value is 4.0, the best prediction for the associated dependent variable (DV) value is 3.1. The third column of Table 9.5 shows all four predictions of the dependent variable values associated with the four known independent variable values. You make all the predictions using the regression equation.

Table 9.5   Coefficient of determination – remaining error

Observed IV values	Observed DV values	Predicted DV values[1]	Prediction errors	Prediction errors squared
1	2	1.3	2 – 1.3 = +0.7	(+0.7) × (+0.7) = 0.49
2	1	1.9	1 – 1.9 = –0.9	(–0.9) × (–0.9) = 0.81
4	3	3.1	3 – 3.1 = –0.1	(–0.1) × (–0.1) = 0.01
5	4	3.7	4 – 3.7 = +0.3	(+0.3) × (+0.3) = 0.09
				Sum of squares = 1.40

$$\text{Variance} = \frac{\text{Sum of squares}}{\text{Number of values}} = \frac{1.40}{4} = 0.35 = \text{Remaining error}$$

[1] Expected DV values calculated using regression equation DV = 0.7 + (0.6 × IV), e.g. when observed IV value = 1, predicted DV value = 0.7 + (0.6 × 1) = 1.3.

However, as the *Prediction errors* column of Table 9.5 shows, when you compare the predicted values of the dependent variable to the original observed values, there are still prediction errors. These errors make up the remaining error. In other words, they are the errors that remain after predicting the values of the dependent variable *with* knowledge of the values of the independent variable. You use the variance of these prediction errors as a single-figure measure of the remaining error. As Table 9.5 shows, in this example the remaining error is 0.35.

With an original error of 1.25 and a remaining error of 0.35, the proportional reduction in error, and thus the coefficient of determination, is as follows:

$$\begin{array}{l}\text{Coefficient of} \\ \text{determination}\end{array} = \frac{\text{Original error} - \text{Remaining error}}{\text{Original error}} = \frac{1.25 - 0.35}{1.25} = 0.72$$

You interpret the coefficient of determination in exactly the same way as the lambda coefficient from Chapter 8. The coefficient of determination can vary between 0 and 1, where 0 represents a zero correlation and 1 represents a perfect correlation. A value of 0.72 means that knowledge of the independent variable leads to a reduction in error of 72% when predicting values of the dependent variable. In other words, there is a strong correlation between the two variables.

So far, the section has used very simple data to illustrate how to calculate a coefficient of determination. However, exactly the same steps apply to a larger data set, such as that about happiness and social integration. Table 9.6 shows these steps. Thus, without knowledge of the Integration values, the best prediction of each Happiness value is the mean (152.9). The difference between each Happiness value and the predicted mean value represents the error in each prediction. A single-figure measure of this error is the variance value (601.7). Thus, 601.7 is the original error. The next step is to make predictions of the Happiness values using the regression equation:

Happiness = 74.6 + (0.432 × Integration)

As before, the difference between each prediction and the actual value represents the prediction error. A single-figure measure of this error is the variance value (130.6). Thus, 130.6 is the remaining error.

Table 9.6   Coefficient of determination – Happiness and Integration

Step	Statistic	Values
1	Mean of Happiness (DV)	152.9
2	Original error (variance of prediction errors using Happiness mean)	601.7
3	Remaining error (variance of prediction errors using regression equation)	130.6
4	Proportional reduction in error	0.78

The final step is to calculate the coefficient of determination. It's a proportional reduction in error measure, and calculated in the usual way:

$$\text{Coefficient of determination} = \frac{\text{Original error} - \text{Remaining error}}{\text{Original error}} = \frac{601.7 - 130.6}{601.7} = 0.78$$

A coefficient of determination of 0.78 tells you that the prediction error goes down by 78% when predicting Happiness values *with* knowledge of Integration values compared to making these predictions *without* knowledge of the Integration values. It shows that there is a strong correlation between the two variables, Happiness and Integration.

Eta-squared correlation coefficient

Up to now the book has discussed numerical variables and categorical variables in different chapters. However, this section looks at both types of variable together. It explains the thinking behind measuring the strength of a correlation or association between one numerical variable and one categorical variable using a coefficient called *eta squared*. (*Eta* is the letter *H* in the Greek alphabet.) It is another proportional reduction in error measure, and so the only difference from the previous coefficient is in the detail of calculating the original and remaining errors.

$$\text{Eta-squared coefficient} = \frac{\text{Original error} - \text{Remaining error}}{\text{Original error}}$$

Work involving both numerical and categorical data is quite common. For example, a lecturing team may be interested in how well male students do compared to female students. The table below shows the exam results of a small sample of nine men and nine women.

Female	70	65	60	65	80	70	70	75	75
Male	63	71	63	67	55	59	67	63	50

The researcher thus knows two things about each student (i.e. each unit of analysis):

1 His or her sex (i.e. female, male)
2 His or her exam result (e.g. 70, 63).

There are thus two variables. Sex is a categorical variable with two categories (Male and Female). It's the independent variable. The dependent variable, Exam result, is a numerical variable. Recall that an association exists when your knowledge of the values of the independent variable allows you to predict more accurately the values of the dependent variable. So, you want to measure the degree to which knowing whether each student is male or female helps improve your predictions of their exam results.

When the independent variable has only two categories, the easiest way to think about the association is in terms of the *difference* in exam scores between men and women. The bigger the difference, the stronger the correlation between the variables. This is because using information about the male group will result in a more accurate prediction about the exam score of each male student, and using information about the female group will result in a more accurate prediction of the exam score of each female student.

Eta squared is a proportional reduction in error measure. Thus, to work out the coefficient value you need a measure of the original error and the remaining error. The original error is based on the difference between the mean exam mark for *all* students (66.5) and the original mark of each student. As in the previous example, a one-figure summary of these differences is measured by the variance. Table 9.7 shows that the variance, and thus the original error, is 39.6.

You now measure the remaining error – the error that remains when you predict values of the dependent variable (Exam) *with* knowledge of the values of the independent variable (Sex). These predictions are based on the mean of each *category*, not the overall mean. As Table 9.8 shows, for each man the best prediction is the male mean (63.0), and for each woman the best prediction is the female

Table 9.7   Eta-squared correlation coefficient – original error

Observed DV values	Predicted DV values[1]	Prediction errors	Prediction errors squared
Women			
70	66.5	3.5	12.25
65	66.5	−1.5	2.25
60	66.5	−6.5	42.25
65	66.5	−1.5	2.25
80	66.5	13.5	182.25
70	66.5	3.5	12.25
70	66.5	3.5	12.25
75	66.5	8.5	72.25
75	66.5	8.5	72.25
Men			
63	66.5	−3.5	12.25
71	66.5	4.5	20.25
63	66.5	−3.5	12.25
67	66.5	0.5	0.25
55	66.5	−11.5	132.25
59	66.5	−7.5	56.25
67	66.5	0.5	0.25
63	66.5	−3.5	12.25
59	66.5	−7.5	56.25
			Sum of squares = 712.50

$$\text{Variance} = \frac{\text{Sum of squares}}{\text{Number of values}} = \frac{712.5}{18} = 39.6 = \text{Original error}$$

[1] Predicted DV values is Exam mean for *all* students.

mean (70.0). As before, a one-figure summary of these differences is measured by the variance. The remaining error is a measure of the differences between these predictions and the observed values. Table 9.8(c) shows that the overall remaining error is 27.3.

Thus, the original error is 39.6 and the remaining error is 27.3. The final step is to calculate the proportional reduction in error in the usual way:

$$\text{Eta-squared correlation coefficient} = \frac{\text{Original error} - \text{Remaining error}}{\text{Original error}}$$

$$= \frac{39.6 - 27.3}{39.6} = 0.31$$

Table 9.8 Eta-squared correlation coefficient – remaining error

Table 9.8(a): Women

Observed DV values	Predicted DV values	Prediction errors	Prediction errors squared
70	66.5	0	0
65	66.5	−5	25
60	66.5	−10	100
65	66.5	−5	25
80	66.5	10	100
70	66.5	0	0
70	66.5	0	0
75	66.5	5	25
75	66.5	5	25
			Sum of squares = 300

$$\text{Variance} = \frac{\text{Sum of squares}}{\text{Number of values}} = \frac{300}{9} = 33.3 = \text{Remaining error (women)}$$

Table 9.8(b): Men

Observed DV values	Predicted DV values	Prediction errors	Prediction errors squared
63	63	0	0
71	63	8	64
63	63	0	0
67	63	4	16
55	63	−8	64
59	63	−4	16
67	63	4	16
63	63	0	0
59	63	−4	16
			Sum of squares = 192

$$\text{Variance} = \frac{\text{Sum of squares}}{\text{Number of values}} = \frac{192}{9} = 21.3 = \text{Remaining error (men)}$$

Table 9.8(c): Women and men combined

Women's remaining error	33.3
Men's remaining error	21.3
Overall remaining error	(33.3 + 21.3) ÷ 2 = 27.3

A coefficient of 0.31 tells you that the error is reduced by 31% when predicting exam values knowing whether each student is a man or woman compared to making these predictions without knowing each student's sex. In other words, it shows that there is a moderate correlation between the two variables, Exam and Sex.

Direction of correlations

The above sections show how to measure the *strength* of a correlation between two variables. This section focuses on the *direction* of the correlation. Basically, this is about whether the regression line on a scattergraph slopes up or down. Figure 9.5(a) shows a regression line sloping upwards, and Figure 9.5(b) shows a regression line sloping downwards.

IV	1	2	3	4	5	6	7	8	9	10
DV	2	4	6	8	10	12	14	16	18	20

IV	1	2	3	4	5	6	7	8	9	10
DV	20	18	16	14	12	10	8	6	4	2

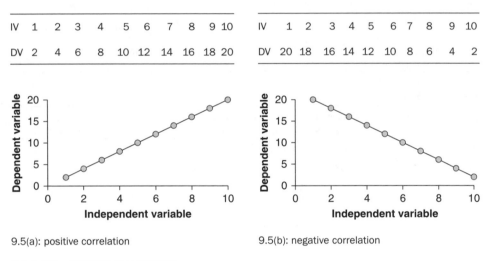

9.5(a): positive correlation

9.5(b): negative correlation

Figure 9.5   Direction of correlations

The regression line in Figure 9.5(a) goes up and to the right, away from where the two axes meet. This indicates that as the values of the independent variable increase, so too do the values of the dependent variable. The regression equation for this data is DV = 0 + (2.0 × IV). For example, plugging in an independent variable value of 4 gives the following: DV = 0 + (2.0 × 4) = 8. Notice that the equation includes a plus (+) sign. When the dependent values increase as the independent values increase, there is a *positive* correlation between the two variables. One real-world example of a positive correlation is between house size and house price. Generally, large houses sell for a higher price than small houses.

Not all correlations are positive ones. For example, the regression line in Figure 9.5(b) slopes downward, indicating that as the values of the independent variable increase, those of the dependent variable decrease. The regression equation for this set of data is DV = 22 – (2.0 × IV). For example, plugging in an independent variable value of 4 gives the following: DV = 22 – (2.0 × 4) = 14. Notice that the equation includes a minus (–) sign. When the dependent values decrease as the independent values increase, there is a *negative* correlation between the two variables. One real-world example of a negative correlation is between altitude and air pressure: the higher the altitude, the lower the air pressure (that's why most climbers on Mount Everest carry oxygen bottles).

A coefficient of determination focuses on the strength of a correlation, the value showing the proportional reduction in prediction errors. But it doesn't show the direction of the association. You have to look at the trend of points on the scattergraph, or at the sign (+ or −) in the regression equation, to identify the direction of the association. However, other coefficients do show the direction of the association. One of the best known is *Pearson's correlation coefficient*, named after its originator, the British statistician Karl Pearson.

BEHIND THE STATS

Karl Pearson (1857–1936) developed the earlier regression work of Francis Galton. Despite being a very productive researcher (producing over 500 papers and books), Pearson also took on heavy teaching commitments at the University of London. He was able to do both, he said, because he never answered a telephone or attended a committee meeting – advice that many academics today would dearly like to follow! See Tankard (1984: Ch. 4).

Pearson's correlation coefficient varies between +1 and −1. A perfect positive correlation, such as that in Figure 9.5(a), has a Pearson score of +1.0. A perfect negative correlation, such as that shown in Figure 9.5(b), has a Pearson score of −1.0. The only time that a Pearson coefficient does not have a positive or negative sign is when there is a zero correlation.

Don't get confused between the descriptions of the *strength* of the correlation (perfect to zero) and the *direction* of the correlation (positive and negative). A *perfect negative* correlation is not a contradiction in terms. It occurs: (i) when the predictions of the dependent variable values are perfectly accurate; and (ii) when the dependent variable values go down as the independent variable values go up.

In fact, Pearson's correlation coefficient is simply the square root of the coefficient of determination. The advantage of using the coefficient of determination is that it is a proportional reduction in error measure. In other words, it directly shows how much prediction error is lost when using the independent variable values. For example, a coefficient of 0.50 means a 50% reduction in error. You cannot interpret Pearson's correlation coefficient in the same way. You have to *square* the Pearson value to get this information. When squaring values less than 1, you end up with a result that is smaller than the original. For example, squaring a Pearson's correlation coefficient of 0.7 gives a coefficient of determination of 0.49 (0.7×0.7). Thus, a Pearson coefficient of 0.7 means a reduction in prediction error of 49%.

Finally, what can you say about the direction of an association between a categorical and numerical variable? If the categorical variable has only two categories, then it's always possible to compare categories. In the previous example about exam results and the sex of students, the strength of the correlation was measured using eta squared (0.31). The direction of the correlation is reflected in the difference between the category means. The average exam score of the men is 63%, and the average exam score of the women is 70%. Thus, the direction of the association is that the women score *better* than the men. However, if there are more than two categories, then the idea of the direction of the association does not apply because the categories do not have any in-built order.

Nature of correlations

So far the focus has been on fitting a *straight* line to summarise the pattern of points on a scattergraph. This is because it is much easier to work out the regression equation for a straight line than for a curved line – after all, you need to join up only two points on a graph when using a straight line. However, straight lines are not always the most appropriate summary lines. Other associations are best described by curved lines, and are known, not surprisingly, as *curvilinear associations*.

Figure 9.6 shows a positive correlation between stopping distance and travelling speed: the greater the speed, the longer the stopping distance. But a straight line is not the best way to describe the correlation because stopping distance does not increase steadily with speed. An increase of 10 km/h or 5 mph at a higher speed produces a much longer stopping distance than the same 10 km/h or 5 mph increase at a lower speed. Thus, the correlation between stopping distance and speed is curvilinear.

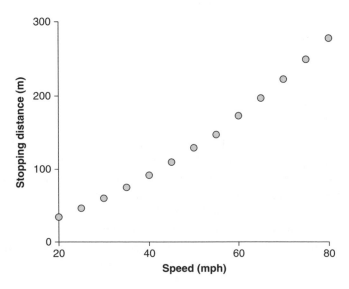

Figure 9.6   Curvilinear correlation: stopping distance, by speed
Source: Based on data in AASHTO 2004: 112

There are even more complex curves. For example, Blanchflower and Oswald (2008) show that there is a U-shaped curve between age and happiness. Never try to fit a straight line onto a scatter of points that suggests a curvilinear correlation between the variables. It's like trying to fit a square peg into a round hole.

This long chapter has covered a lot of ground. If researchers are to explain why things occur, then establishing that there is a correlation between two variables is one of the essential elements of numerical analysis. The following chapters take a different approach, and look at what researchers do when, as is usually the case, they are working with only a small part of the group of people they are interested in studying.

Part Four

Sampling and estimation

TEN

Introducing sampling

Chapter Overview

This chapter will:

- Provide an overview on how social researchers collect data from the social world by *sampling*.
- Introduce some concepts that underpin sampling – *population*, *sampling frame*, *sampling pool*, and *sample*.
- Show that *probability sampling* depends on chance alone to select the sample, and is the basis of much subsequent analysis where researchers use the results from the sample to make inferences about the population.
- Show that *non-probability sampling*, which does not depend on chance alone to select the sample, has much more limited research use.

Most researchers are interested in groups that are much too large for them to study as a whole. For example, public opinion pollsters hired to predict the result of the next national election could not possibly ask all the millions of voters about their voting intentions. Indeed, given the amount of money available to carry out the research, it is not possible to get in touch with all the hundreds of thousands of voters to predict the outcome of a small state election, or even the tens of thousands of voters to predict a local government election.

It follows, therefore, that researchers interested in large groups have to base their research on the results from smaller, more manageable groups. Each smaller group is termed a *sample*. As far as possible, the sample should be representative of the much larger group (the *population*). Thus, public opinion pollsters first measure the voting intentions of the people in the sample. They then use the sample results to predict the likely voting intentions of all the people in the population. However, you can find the *exact* intentions of all voters in the population only when you ask them all (and they all give you honest answers!). What you can do with the sample results is to *infer* from them the most likely or most probable population results. Statistics used to infer the most probable population results are termed *inferential statistics*.

This and the next two chapters look at sampling and inferential statistics. This chapter focuses on sampling. It's important, of course, because even the

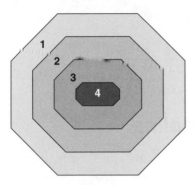

1 **Population** All individuals of interest in survey area
2 **Sampling frame** List of contact details for all individuals
3 **Sampling pool** Individuals invited to participate
4 **Sample** Individuals who do participate

Figure 10.1   Sampling jargon

best statistical analysis is not worth much if it uses bad data. The quality of the data in part depends on how the researchers select the sample from the population.

Most sampling involves going through the series of stages shown in Figure 10.1. Try to see this diagram as a series of superimposed shapes of decreasing size, with the largest representing the population, and the smallest representing the sample. The rest of the chapter looks in turn at the four stages shown in Figure 10.1, starting with the population.

Population

The first step in sampling is always to have a clear idea about the *population*. As Leslie Kish notes in his classic book, *Survey Sampling*, 'the population is the aggregate of the elements, and the elements are the basic units that comprise and define the population' (1965: 7). Researchers identify the *sampling elements* by asking exactly who is the focus of the research. The population is identified by the geographical or social boundaries that define the location of the sampling elements.

For example, you are interested in voters in a particular local government election. The sampling elements are people who are eligible to vote. The population is defined by the boundaries of this local government election. The boundaries are largely geographical, but could also be social as, for example, when someone lives elsewhere but owns property in the area and, according to local laws, is therefore eligible to vote.

Sampling frame

The next level of Figure 10.1 is the *sampling frame*. The ideal sampling frame is a list of the names and contact details of all elements in the population. For example, a local social club asks you to conduct a survey of its members. The secretary provides you with a membership list of 1000 names and contact details that he assures you is both complete and up to date. If the list is as good as the secretary says, then it's an ideal sampling frame. (Unfortunately, the life of a researcher is rarely this easy!)

Sampling frames almost invariably include *coverage errors*. *Undercoverage* occurs when elements in the population are missing from the sampling frame. Not surprisingly, *overcoverage* occurs when elements that are not part of the population are included in the sampling frame. Undercoverage is usually the more important type of error. Imagine, for example, a study of teenage drug use that uses enrolment lists from the local high schools. This sampling frame leaves out students who have left school early. Behaviour patterns, including drug use, among these missing sampling elements may be very different from teenagers who are still at school and thus in the sampling frame. Overall, researchers need to find out as much as possible about their sampling frame to identify coverage errors.

Sampling pool

The sampling frame is the link between the theoretical population and the practical *sampling pool* – those people on the sampling frame asked to participate in the survey. Survey researchers have two basic methods of selecting individuals from the sampling frame for inclusion in the sampling pool: probability sampling and non-probability sampling.

Probability sampling

In probability sampling, you know the probability of each element being in the sampling pool. You can then analyse the results using inferential statistics to make definite statements about the population. To do this, you need to make sure that selection into the sampling pool depends *on chance alone*. In other words, you have to make the sampling procedure completely objective. If you have seen a lottery draw on TV you have seen probability sampling in action. The several dozen numbered balls represent the population. The container spins to mix them to make sure that each ball has an equal chance of selection. Because the machine catches each ball at random, the method is known as *random sampling*.

Similarly, often the first step in probability sampling is to number each element on the sampling frame. However, the marvellous machine used on TV is replaced with something much more down to earth – a table of random numbers (or its electronic equivalent). As Table 10.1 shows, this is simply a list of numbers with no pattern to the order in which they appear. Tables of random

Table 10.1   Random numbers table

290	943	714	087	596	923	429	897	164	401
534	317	869	220	101	699	143	189	994	942
749	622	839	665	991	497	642	120	892	061
153	283	395	426	944	106	433	349	680	184
912	549	236	843	004	541	203	197	685	308

numbers often appear in statistics textbooks, or you can make your own with statistical software.

For example, the section on sampling frames above refers to a membership list of 1000 names provided by the secretary of a local social club. To allow random sampling to take place, each name needs a unique number, from 000 to 999 (so that all 1000 numbers have three digits). You then use the table of random numbers to select a simple random sample. The easiest way is to go to the start of the table and then read off the numbers either across or down the list (it doesn't matter which). Reading across Table 10.1, the first number is 290, the second is 943, and the third 714. Thus, the members of the sampling frame numbered 290, 943, and 714 are the first to go into the sampling pool. You continue going through the list until you have the required number of people.

Basic simple random sampling can be a time-consuming process, and researchers usually use quicker techniques for probability sampling. For example, *systematic random* sampling involves going to a point at random in the random numbers table, and then selecting numbers at a fixed interval on the sampling frame. For example, to select 100 names from 1000, you need to select 1 in 10 names. Identify the first value on the random number table (i.e. 290) and find the person on the sampling frame with that number. Then select every 10th name at regular intervals until you have 100 names (i.e. 290th, 300th, 310th ...).

Another probability sampling technique is *stratified random* sampling. This takes place when you can divide a sampling frame into groups (or *strata*) based on a characteristic that you believe is important to the research. For example, men and women often differ in their attitudes, behaviours, and so on. Gender, therefore, is one characteristic often used to stratify a sampling frame. If you want to draw a sample of 100 stratified by gender from the social club's membership list, the first task is to divide the sampling frame into two separate lists, one for men and the other for women. You then draw a systematic random sample as before. Stratifying the sampling frame ensures that exactly the same proportions of men and women are in the sample pool as there are in the sampling frame.

Of course, the sampling frame has to include the information to allow you to place all individuals into strata. For example, if the social club's list has an honorific next to each name (e.g. Mr J Smith), then assigning members to the male or female list is straightforward. If the list gives the full names of members, then the sex of most of them will be clear (e.g. John Smith). But if only the family name is in full, then you can't stratify by gender (e.g. J Smith).

Non-probability sampling

So far, the chapter has focused on different types of probability sampling. However, there is another set of techniques, called *non-probability* sampling. The general characteristic of these techniques is that membership of the sampling pool is decided subjectively by the researchers or respondents, rather than objectively using random numbers. If they use non-probability sampling, researchers do not know the probability of each person being in the sampling pool. As a result, they cannot make definite statements about the population.

Convenience (or *availability*) sampling is the most common type of non-probability sampling. Rather than contacting specific individuals, researchers put out a general invitation to participate, often via the media. For example, my daily newspaper invites readers to answer a question by ringing either a 'Yes' or 'No' number. My favourite question is 'Are Rafael Nadal's tennis shorts too long?'

BEHIND THE STATS

A few decades ago, Nadal's long shorts would have been too short at Wimbledon, as it wasn't until the 1940s that men were allowed to play in tennis shorts (Atkin 2008). In women's tennis, players originally wore heavy, non-revealing clothing, including a bustle, a hat, and sometimes a fur. In 1887, Lottie Dod (UK) was allowed to wear a calf-length skirt – but only because it was part of 16-year-old Lottie's school uniform. It wasn't until 1919 that Suzanne Lenglen (France) wore a calf-length frock. The first woman to play in shorts on the centre court at Wimbledon was Bunny Austin (USA) in 1933 (i.e. a decade or so before men). Wimbledon tightened its clothing rules in 2006 – though this was probably as much to do with the maximum size of sponsors' logos as the minimum size of players' clothes.

The fundamental problem with a procedure that relies on the self-selection of members to the sample is working out exactly which people the respondents *represent*. For example, to what degree are readers of a newspaper representative of everyone living in the newspaper's circulation area? And to what degree are survey respondents representative of this newspaper's readers? Usually, self-selected respondents have more strongly held opinions than the general population. After all, it's easier *not* to take part, and the less strong your opinion, the less strong your motivation to participate.

Another non-probability technique is *snowball* sampling. It's based on the simple idea that many people in a small population that is scattered throughout the general community will know someone else from the same group, and may be prepared to give contact details to the researchers. Snowball sampling is especially useful if members of the special population are stigmatised, such as those seen as sexually deviant. In these cases, researchers begin by becoming known and trusted by those who organise group events. They then extend the research beyond this initial group by snowball sampling. Figure 10.2 shows an example. An initial set of contacts leads researchers to other people, some of whom, in turn, introduce the researchers to yet others in the survey population.

The section began with the comment that non-probability sampling does not allow researchers to make definite statements about the population. This leads to the basic question of why on earth would anyone want to use non-probability sampling? In terms of many of the surveys you see in the media, a newspaper or

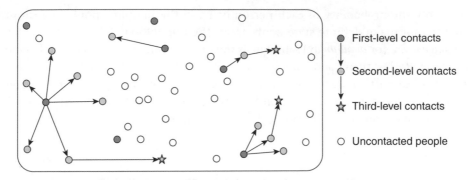

Figure 10.2   Snowball sampling

TV company is less interested in how the survey is done than in the potential to use the results as a news item. (Nadal's tennis shorts come to mind here!) This being the case, the ease and cheapness of non-probability sampling are often the deciding factors. But what about academic and other more serious surveys?

First, researchers often use non-probability sampling when *developing* question-naires. Thus, at the very early stages, researchers do exploratory work to give them a basic understanding of the key issues in the research. For example, they may use non-probability sampling to test the best wording of questions and the range of possible answers. Finding a representative sample is not a prime concern.

Second, non-probability sampling such as snowball sampling is also valuable when a sampling frame is not available and the population is a very small propor-tion of the general population. The problem is made worse if the survey topic is a sensitive one because people will be less likely to give honest answers. Sometimes, respondents will give honest answers only when researchers distrib-ute the questionnaires through intermediaries, thus guaranteeing respondents' anonymity. But, of course, the less control researchers have over the sampling process, the less sure they can be about the probability of any individual being in the survey.

Sample

The smallest shape in Figure 10.1 is the *sample* – the people who actually take part in the survey. It's the information provided by these people that allows researchers to describe the population. Of course, not everyone in the sampling pool will end up in the sample. The researchers may not be able to track down some people. And some people who are contacted will refuse to take part. The percentage of those in the sampling pool who are contacted and agree to take part is referred to as the *response rate*. This varies with a number of factors. For exam-ple, how researchers ask the questions is important, with face-to-face surveys usu-ally getting a better response rate than mail surveys. The focus of the questions is also important, with those asking about generally acceptable behaviours getting a better response rate than those asking about socially unacceptable activities. The higher the response rate, the more confident you can be that the sample reflects the population.

BEHIND THE STATS

Charles Cannell (1985) tells the following story about survey research:

> One of our interviewers called a random number and somebody answered the phone and said, *'Yes, who is this calling?'* The interviewer said, 'This is the University of Michigan, Survey Research Center.' *'What are you calling about?'* 'Well we are doing a survey.' *'How did you get this number?'* 'It is random digit dialling.' *'Who did you say was calling?'* The interviewer got slightly annoyed and said: 'It is the University of Michigan, but why are you asking me all those questions?' *'Madam, you have reached a number in the Pentagon that no one is supposed to know anything about.'* As well as the Pentagon part of the story, I particularly enjoyed the rather peevish response from the survey interviewer – 'but why are you asking me all these questions?'!

However, even when researchers carefully follow every step of the sampling process, the only way they can be absolutely sure that survey results precisely reflect the population is to persuade *everyone* in the population to take part – a practical impossibility. Given that this is not possible, you need to consider the effect of different sample sizes on estimates of population values. This involves using *sampling distributions* and *standard errors*. These basic statistical concepts are the focus of the next two chapters.

ELEVEN

Estimating numbers

Chapter Overview

This chapter will:
- Provide an overview on how to estimate the population mean based on a sample mean.
- Show how samples of the same size drawn from the same population will give different mean results. Together, these are called the *sampling distribution of the means*.
- Show how, by using the mean and standard deviation of the known sample, you can use the sampling distribution to estimate the mean of the unknown population.
- Highlight the importance of the sample size when estimating the population mean.

As the previous chapter showed, researchers who are interested in large populations have to base their research on the results from smaller, more manageable samples. As far as possible, the sample should be representative of the population. However, you can describe the population *exactly* only if you survey everyone in it. What you can do with the sample result is to infer from it the most probable population result using *inferential statistics*.

There are two basic types of analysis using inferential statistics: *estimation* and *hypothesis testing*. They involve looking at the sample data from different perspectives, like describing a glass as 'half-full' or 'half-empty'. This and the next chapter focus on estimation – how to estimate population values such as means and percentages from sample results. This chapter is about numerical data – measuring variables with numbers. The following chapter goes through the same ideas but with categorical data.

Variability in sample results

Inferential statistics work with samples that, as far as possible, are representative of the population. This means that you use inferential statistics with data collected using probability sampling. As Chapter 10 pointed out, with probability sampling every individual in the population has a known probability (i.e. chance) of being in the sample. Researchers select individuals at random, using a random numbers table.

Unfortunately, even probability sampling cannot *guarantee* a sample that exactly reflects the population from which it is drawn. The following very simple set of numbers illustrates this:

❶ ❸ ❺ ❼ ❾

You paint each number on a ball and place the five balls in the lottery drum. These numbered balls make up the population. The machine randomly picks out one ball, you make a note of its number (e.g. 3), replace it, wait for the machine to pick out a second ball, and again note its number (e.g. 5). These two selections make up a sample. You then work out the mean of the two numbers in the sample (i.e. 4). As the population mean is 5 (i.e. $(1 + 3 + 5 + 7 + 9) \div 5$), you might also expect a similar sample mean. However, although a mean of 5 is the most *likely* result, it is not the only one. Altogether there are nine possible sample means (1, 2, 3, 4, 5, 6, 7, 8, and 9), though some are more likely to occur than others. For example, there is only one way of getting a sample mean of 1 – drawing 1, replacing it, and then drawing 1 again. There are two ways of getting a sample mean of 2 (1 + 3 and 3 + 1). And there are three ways of getting a sample mean of 3 (1 + 5, 3 + 3, and 5 + 1). Figure 11.1 shows all 25 possible results.

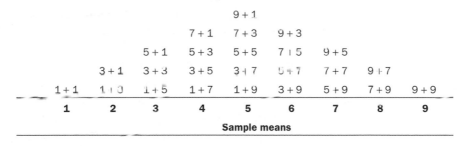

Figure 11.1　All possible sample results: sampling two values from a population of five values (1, 3, 5, 7, 9)

Figure 11.2 summarises this information about the sample results. The graph shows a *sampling distribution*, so called because it is the distribution of all possible sample results for the same sample size.

The sampling distribution shows three important things:

1 Most importantly, the sampling distribution is centred on the actual population mean (i.e. 5)
2 The sample result in the centre of the distribution is also the sample result most likely to occur. The greater the difference between the population and the sample result, the smaller the chance of drawing such a sample.
3 The sampling distribution is symmetrical. In other words, the left-hand side of the graph is a mirror image of the right-hand side.

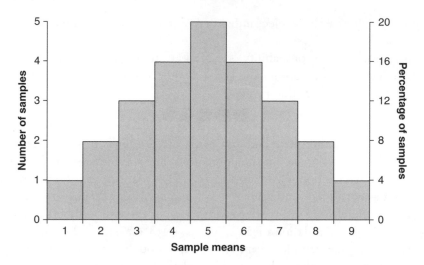

Figure 11.2   Sampling distribution: sampling two values from a population of five values (1, 3, 5, 7, 9)

These general features also apply to much larger studies. For example, a university careers adviser carries out a survey of 225 of the 10,000 recent graduates, and finds that the mean salary of the sample is $50,000. What does this sample result say about the salaries of *all* recent graduates from the university? The *most likely* sample value is also the actual population value. Thus, provided the survey used probability sampling, the best single estimate of the population mean is the one given by the sample result – $50,000. A best single estimate is termed a *point estimate*.

However, to leave the analysis there ignores the fact that each sample is only one of a much larger number of possible samples. Thus, the result from the one sample taken is just one of a much larger number of possible results. Although the most likely sample result is the actual population value, there is no guarantee that the result from the one sample taken is the population value.

Your analysis needs to take into account this variability in sample results. The reasoning is similar to that about the mean and the standard deviation. The descriptive power of the mean depends on how spread out the distribution is around the mean. In other words, it depends on the variability of the values around the mean, as measured by the standard deviation. Similarly, what you need here is not only the result from the one sample taken, but also a measure of the variability of all possible results from samples of the same size as the one sample taken. In other words, you need to know the standard deviation of the means for all possible samples of the same size as yours.

With the previous very small example, it was easy to work out all the possible samples, calculate the sample mean, and draw up the sampling distribution. This isn't possible with real-life research where the only information you have comes from a single sample. The following section shows how to *estimate* population values from the results of just a single sample.

Variability in sample results – a real-life example

In the graduate salary survey referred to above, there are 225 graduates in the sample and 10,000 graduates in the population. This means that there are many millions of different samples of 225 graduates in addition to the one taken. Even if you have the computing power to calculate all the sample means, you still face an impossible task because you do not know the salaries of all 10,000 graduates in the population. And if you knew all the salaries, there would be absolutely no point in taking a sample!

Fortunately, you don't need to do the impossible, and draw the many millions of different samples of 225 graduates from the population of 10,000, calculate the mean salary of each, and then plot all the means on a bar graph. Drawing on work done by statisticians, you can accurately *predict* what the sampling distribution of salary means looks like. Figure 11.3 shows this sampling distribution. It's called a *normal distribution* because the same type of bell-shaped graph is normally produced when you plot the distribution of all the results from samples of the same large size.

BEHIND THE STATS

The first person to identify a normal distribution was Abraham de Moivre (1667–1754). At the time, writers did not take spelling too seriously, spelling even their own names in several ways. For example, Abraham at different times spelled his family name as de *Moivre*, *Demoivre*, and *De Moivre* (Tankard 1984: 146). A century earlier, attitudes to spelling were even more lax. For example, Shakespeare (1564–1616) 'did not spell his name the same way twice in any of his six known signatures, and even spelled it two ways on one document, his will …. Curiously, the one spelling he never seemed to use himself was *Shakespeare*' (Bryson 1990: 116).

It is extremely important that you understand Figure 11.3 because the idea of sampling distributions runs through much of the rest of the book. Remember, Figure 11.3 shows the results of all the millions of possible different samples of 225 graduates that can be taken from the population of 10,000 graduates. For each sample, you calculate the mean of the 225 salaries, and plot it along with the millions of other sample means. The horizontal axis shows sample means. Those samples with the lowest means (i.e. when, by chance, only the most poorly paid graduates in the population are sampled) are in the bars on the left. Those samples with the highest means (i.e. when, by chance, only the most highly paid graduates in the population are sampled) are in the bars on the right. The vertical axis shows the percentage of samples with each of the various sample mean results. The taller the bar, the greater the percentage of samples with this mean result. Figure 11.4 summarises the basic steps in building a sampling distribution.

The features of the sampling distribution of the very simple example shown in Figure 11.2 also apply to the sampling distribution for the millions of samples

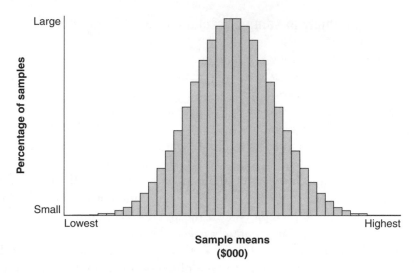

Figure 11.3   A 'normal' sampling distribution

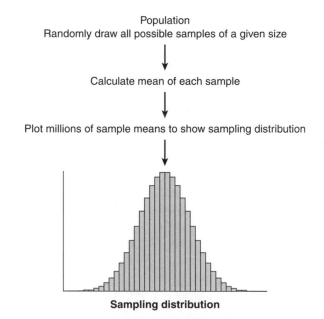

Figure 11.4   Logic of sampling distribution of means

about graduate salaries. First, it is centred on the actual population mean – the average salary of all 10,000 recent graduates. For example, if the careers adviser had surveyed *all* 10,000 graduates and found that the population mean was $50,000, then the sampling distribution of salary means would be centred on $50,000.

Second, it is centred on the sample result that is most likely to occur – the bars are tallest in the centre of the distribution. Thus, the samples that are most likely to occur are those showing a mean value equal to the population mean.

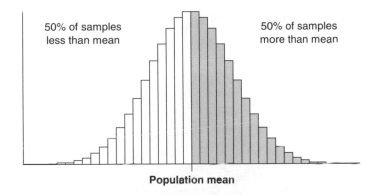

50% of samples less than mean

50% of samples more than mean

Population mean

Third, it is symmetrical – the left side is a mirror image of the right. Consequently, the umpteen million samples with means that are *less* than the population mean are matched by the same number of umpteen million samples with means that are *more* than the population mean. In fact, you can give a much more detailed description of the normal distribution. To make the following account easier to understand, assume that you already know the mean ($50,000) and the standard deviation ($10,000) of the sampling distribution of the salaries. However, it is important to bear in mind that I have simply plucked these figures out of the air. Indeed, the whole purpose of this section is to *estimate* the mean of the sampling distribution, and from there to *estimate* the population mean.

Table 11.1 shows six salary categories based on a mean of $50,000 and a standard deviation of $10,000. It is centred on $50,000 and moves away from it in units of $10,000 (i.e. in standard deviation units). To simplify things, assume that no sample result is *exactly* the same as the population mean ($50,000.00) or any other values used to divide up the categories (e.g. $60,000.00, $40,000.00).

Table 11.1   Chance of sample means occurring in sampling distribution

Sample means ($)[1]	Chances of occurring
Under 30,000	2½%
Over 30,000 to under 40,000	13½%
Over 40,000 to under 50,000	34%
Over 50,000 to under 60,000	34%
Over 60,000 to under 70,000	13½%
Over 70,000	2½%

[1] If mean of sampling distribution is $50,000 and standard deviation is $10,000.

Table 11.1 also shows the likelihood of sample results occurring in each category. For example, there is a 34% chance of drawing a sample with a mean over $50,000 and under $60,000; a 13½% chance of drawing a sample with a mean over $60,000 and under $70,000; and only a 2½% chance of drawing a sample with a mean of over $70,000. Because the distribution is symmetrical, the same percentages also apply to sample means that are less than the population mean. Figure 11.5 also shows this.

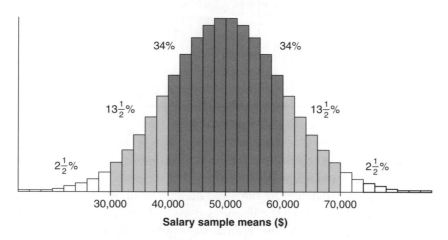

Figure 11.5 Sampling distribution: chance of salary sample means occurring
Note: If mean of sampling distribution is $50,000 and standard deviation is $10,000.

You can standardise the dollar values shown in Figure 11.5 by expressing them in terms of how many 'standard deviation units' they are from the mean. Recall the two statistics plucked out of the air earlier: a mean of $50,000 and a standard deviation of $10,000. Using these figures, you can say that a sample result of $60,000 is $10,000, or one standard deviation unit, more than the mean of the sampling distribution. Because the mean of the sampling distribution is also the population mean, a sample result of $60,000 is one standard deviation unit (i.e. $10,000) more than the population mean, and a sample result of $40,000 is one standard deviation unit less than the population mean. Similarly, $70,000 is two standard deviation units (i.e. $20,000) more than the population mean, and $30,000 is two standard deviation units less than the population mean.

Figure 11.6 replaces the salary sample means shown in Figure 11.5 with standard deviation units. It shows that 68% of all sample means (34 + 34) are within one standard deviation of the population mean. It also shows that 95% (13½ + 34 + 34 + 13½) of all sample means are within two standard deviation units of the population mean. These percentages apply to *all* sampling distributions when the sample size is large enough to produce a normal distribution.

It's now time to get back to the basic problem of how to estimate the population mean based on the result from only one of the huge number of possible samples. The best *single* estimate of the population mean is that given by the one sample result. However, your results need to recognise the variability in sample results. To do this, you need to qualify the mean result from the one sample taken with a measure of this overall variability. A measure of the variability of a distribution is the standard deviation. Thus, the aim is to find the standard deviation of the sampling distribution of the means.

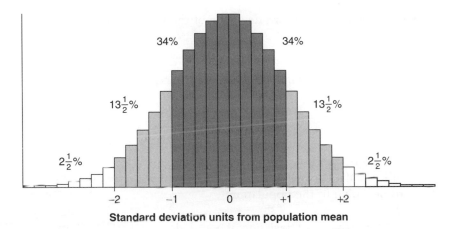

Figure 11.6   Sampling distribution: chance of standardised sample means occurring

Before you can calculate the standard deviation of the sampling distribution, you need to know the standard deviation of the population. And to find the standard deviation of the population, you need to know the population mean – which, of course, is what you were trying to find in the first place! However, statisticians have found a way around this catch-22. It goes like this:

1   Estimate the standard deviation of the population from the standard deviation of the sample:

$$\text{Standard deviation of population} = \text{Standard deviation of sample} \times \sqrt{\frac{\text{Size of sample}}{\text{Size of sample} - 1}}$$

2   Estimate the standard deviation of the sampling distribution of the means from the standard deviation of the population:

$$\text{Standard deviation of sampling distribution of means} = \frac{\text{Standard deviation of population}}{\sqrt{\text{Size of sample}}}$$

The standard deviation of the sampling distribution of the means is usually referred to as the *standard error* of the sample means. This helps to distinguish it from the observed standard deviation of the one sample taken and the estimated standard deviation of the population. The term *standard error* also highlights the fact that it measures the error likely when estimating the population mean from the sample mean. I'll use the term standard error from now on.

How do these two steps apply to the graduate salaries example? There are 225 individuals in the one sample taken. Results from this sample show that the mean of the sample is $49,000 and the standard deviation of the sample is $10,477.

First, you estimate the standard deviation of the population from the standard deviation of the sample:

$$\text{Standard deviation of population} = \text{Standard deviation of sample} \times \sqrt{\frac{\text{Size of sample}}{\text{Size of sample} - 1}}$$

$$\text{Standard deviation of population} = 10{,}477 \times \sqrt{\frac{225}{225-1}} = 10{,}500$$

Second, you estimate the standard error (SE) of the sampling distribution from the standard deviation of the population:

$$\text{SE of sampling distribution} = \frac{\text{Standard deviation of population}}{\sqrt{\text{Size of sample}}} = \frac{10{,}500}{\sqrt{225}} = \frac{10{,}500}{15} = 700$$

The estimate of the standard error of the sampling distribution (i.e. the standard deviation of the sampling distribution) is thus $700.

You now have several useful bits of information about the sampling distribution – that is, about the distribution of the mean salaries of all the millions of possible samples of 225 graduates that can be drawn from the population of 10,000 graduates:

- It has a mean that is the same as the mean of the population from which the samples are drawn.
- It has a standard error of $700.
- It has a normal distribution with all the usual features associated with a normal distribution. For example, 95% of values in the distribution lie within two standard errors of the mean of the sampling distribution – and thus the mean of the population. In this example, two standard errors equals $1400 (i.e. 2 × 700).

Thus, you now know that 95% of all sample means lie within $1400 of the population mean. Consequently, the mean of the one known sample also has a 95% chance of lying within $1400 of the population mean. With an ingenious piece of lateral thinking, you can reverse this statement and say that there's a 95% chance that the population mean lies within $1400 of the mean of the one sample taken. After all, if New York is 1400 miles from Houston, then Houston must be 1400 miles from New York.

If the sample mean is $49,000, then you can be 95% confident that the population mean lies within two standard errors of $49,000. Thus, the population mean lies in the range of the sample mean minus two standard errors ($49,000 – $1400) to the sample mean plus two standard errors ($49,000 + $1400). In other words, you will be correct 95 times in 100 when you say that the population mean (i.e. the mean of all 10,000 graduate salaries) lies within the range of $47,600 to $50,400.

The level of confidence with which you can make this sort of statement is termed (not surprisingly) the *confidence level*. Here, I've used a 95% confidence level. The range of the values within which you are confident the population value will lie is the *confidence interval*. Here, the confidence interval is $2800 ($50,400 minus $47,600). The two ends of the confidence interval ($47,600 and $50,400) are the *confidence limits*.

The above discussion shows how you can go from calculating the mean of a sample ($49,000) to estimating with a given level of confidence (95%) the range of values within which the mean of the population is likely to be found ($47,600 to $50,400). This is termed the *interval estimate*. It is based on the general shape of the sampling distribution of the means, the standard error of which you estimate from the standard deviation of the sample. Table 11.2 summarises this procedure, using the graduate salaries survey as an example.

Table 11.2 Estimating the population mean from a sample mean (e.g. graduate salaries)

Sample (e.g. one sample of 225)	Sampling distribution (e.g. all samples of 225)	Population (e.g. all 10,000 graduates)
1 Calculate mean of sample (e.g. $49,000)		
2 Calculate standard deviation of sample (e.g. $10,477)		
		3 Estimate standard deviation of population (e.g. $10,500)
	4 Estimate standard error of sampling distribution of means (e.g. $700)	
		5 Estimate mean of population
		(a) Point estimate: best single estimate is sample mean (e.g. $49,000)
		(b) Interval estimate = $47,600 to $50,400, i.e. range which you are 95% confident includes population mean is within 2 standard errors (i.e. $1400) of sample mean ($49,000)

Sample size and variability in sample results

It's now time to look briefly at an issue skipped over earlier – the importance of the size of the sample. The graduate salary study is based on quite a large sample of 225 graduates. Consequently, the sampling distribution of the means has a normal shape, is centred on the population mean, and has 95% of sample means within two standard errors of the population mean.

The smaller the sample, the greater the possible difference between the sampling distribution and a normal distribution, and thus the less accurate the population estimate based on a normal distribution. Recall the very simple example with a population of only five values: 1, 3, 5, 7, 9. With a sample size of only 1, sample results of 1, 3, 5, 7, and 9 are equally likely – and thus the sampling distribution of the 'means' does not have a normal shape:

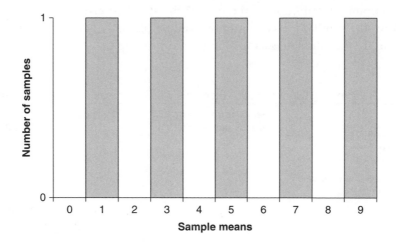

Similarly, with a sample size of 2, the sampling distribution of the means is not normal. However, as Figure 11.2 shows, it does have several characteristics in common with a normal distribution: it is centred on the population mean, it is symmetrical, and it falls away continuously from the centre. But it does not match the precise characteristics of a normal distribution with, for example, 95% of sample means falling within two standard errors of the population mean.

Fortunately, statisticians have calculated the sampling distributions for samples of all sizes. The pioneering work was done by William Gosset, who worked for Guinness Brewery. Gosset's work on small samples stemmed from a very practical concern – how variations in malt and temperature influenced the length of time Guinness remained drinkable. His 'population' was all the Guinness the brewery made, and each of his samples consisted of a number of glasses (or, more likely, test tubes) of Guinness. Each glass needed lengthy analysis to produce a single result, and time restrictions meant that Gosset was often limited to only a few dozen samples (Tankard 1984: Ch. 5). He published his statistical work under the pseudonym 'Student' because Guinness didn't want to publicise his association with the company. Table 11.3 shows some results from Gosset's work on sampling distributions for small sample sizes. They are known as Student's t distributions, though the letter t has no real significance. (Perhaps Student's G might have been more appropriate – for Gosset or Guinness!)

Table 11.3   Sampling distributions for small samples

Sample size	Standard error values enclosing 95% of all sample means
10	2.26
20	2.09
30	2.05
Large	1.96

Table 11.3 is important, and worth looking at carefully. The bottom row refers to large samples. These produce a normal sampling distribution in which 95% of all sample means lie within 1.96 standard errors of the population mean. (Earlier, I rounded off 1.96 to 2 standard errors, but here we need a more precise value.) With a sample size of 30, the sampling distribution is slightly wider than a normal distribution – you have to go out to 2.05 standard errors on either side of the centre to enclose 95% of all sample means. With a sample size of 20, the sampling distribution is wider still, with 95% of all sample means lying within 2.09 standard errors of the population mean. And with a very small sample of only 10, the sampling distribution is even wider, with 95% of all sample means lying within 2.26 standard errors of the population mean.

To estimate the population mean from the mean of one small sample, you use the standard error value in exactly the same way as with large samples. The only difference comes at the end when you work out the 95% confidence interval using the standard error values in Table 11.3. The following example reworks the earlier graduate salary example, but this time using a random sample of only 10 recent graduates rather than 225. For simplicity, assume that the sample mean is still $49,000 and the sample standard deviation is still $10,477.

(i) Standard deviation of population = SD of sample $\times \sqrt{\dfrac{\text{Size of sample}}{\text{Size of sample} -1}}$

$$= 10,477 \times \sqrt{\dfrac{10}{10 - 1}} = 11,044$$

(ii) Standard error of means = $\dfrac{\text{SD of population}}{\sqrt{\text{Size of sample}}} = \dfrac{11,044}{\sqrt{10}} = \dfrac{11,044}{3.16} = 3495$

Using the information from Table 11.3 about the sampling distribution of the means with a sample size of 10, you know that 95% of all sample means lie within 2.26 standard errors of the population mean. The above calculation shows that the standard error is 3495. Thus, you can be 95% confident that the population mean lies between the sample mean minus 2.26 standard errors to the sample mean plus 2.26 standard errors. In other words, you are 95% confident that the population mean lies between $41,101 and $56,899 (i.e. 49,000 – (2.26 × 3495) and 49,000 + (2.26 × 3495)).

The smaller the sample, the wider the confidence interval. For example, with a sample size of 225, you can be 95% confident that the population mean of graduate salaries lies between $47,600 and $50,400, a confidence interval of $2800. In contrast, with a sample size of only 10 the 95% confidence interval is much bigger – $15,798 (i.e. $41,101 to $56,899). This seems reasonable. You can feel more confident about relying on the results of a large sample rather than a small one because a few extreme values are more likely to distort a small sample than a large one.

This chapter looked at how to estimate the mean of a population from the mean of a sample drawn through probability sampling. The next chapter, Chapter 12, covers similar ground, except that it looks at estimating percentages in categorical variables. Chapter 12 has a similar structure to this one. First, it shows how variability is built into the sampling process. Second, it shows how to estimate the population percentage value based on a single sample value. Finally, it highlights the importance of sample size in determining the variability of sample results.

TWELVE

Estimating categories

Chapter Overview

This chapter will:

- Provide an overview on how to estimate a category percentage in a population from a category percentage in a sample.
- Show how samples of the same size drawn from the same population can give different category percentage results. Together, these are called the *sampling distribution of the percentage.*
- Show how, by using the category percentage from the known sample, you can use the sampling distribution to estimate the category percentage of the unknown population.
- Highlight the importance of sample size and variability in sample results when estimating the population percentage.

Chapter 11 looked at how to estimate the mean of a population from the mean of a sample drawn through probability sampling. This chapter covers similar ground, except that it looks at estimating percentages in categorical variables. For example, public opinion pollsters describe the voting intentions of the people in a sample, and from these results describe the likely voting intentions of all the people in the population. However, they can find the *exact* intentions of all voters in the population only by asking them all. What they can do with a sample result is to infer from it the most probable population result using inferential statistics.

This chapter has a similar structure to Chapter 11. First, it shows how variability is built into the sampling process. Second, it shows how to take this variability into account when estimating the population value based on a single sample value. And finally, it highlights the importance of sample size in determining the variability of sample results.

Variability in sample results

Imagine that there are 50 white balls and 50 black balls in a lottery drum. This is the population. The machine picks out a ball, you make a note of its colour, replace it, wait for a second ball to appear, make a note of its colour, replace it, and so on until you have recorded the colours of 6 balls. This is a sample. The use of the machine to pick out the balls means that there is random sampling.

As the population has 50% black balls and 50% white balls, you might expect the same percentage of black and white balls in a sample. However, although the most *likely* result in a sample of 6 balls is 3 black and 3 white, it is by no means the only possible result. Altogether, there are seven possibilities:

- 6 black and 0 white
- 5 black and 1 white
- 4 black and 2 white
- 3 black and 3 white
- 2 black and 4 white
- 1 black and 5 white
- 0 black and 6 white.

There is only 1 way of drawing 6 blacks (BBBBBB) and only 1 way of drawing 6 whites (WWWWWW). But there are 6 ways of drawing 5 blacks and 1 white (WBBBBB, BWBBBB, BBWBBB, BBBWBB, BBBBWB, BBBBBW). Similarly, there are 6 ways of drawing 5 whites and 1 black (BWWWWW, WBWWWW, WWBWWW, WWWBWW, WWWWBW, WWWWWB). Figure 12.1 also shows the 15 ways of drawing 2 blacks and 4 whites; the 15 ways of drawing 2 whites and 4 blacks; and the 20 ways of drawing 3 white balls and 3 black balls. Altogether, there are 64 possible results.

The most likely sample result is 3 black and 3 white – the same as the breakdown of black and white balls in the population. Twenty of the 64 possible combinations contain 3 black and 3 white balls. In other words, this result is likely to occur 31.3% of the time when a sample of 6 is taken from this population in which half the balls are black and half are white. The greater the difference between the population and the sample result, the smaller the chance that you will draw such a sample. Thus, there is a 23.4% chance of either 2 black and 4 white, or 4 black and 2 white; a 9.4% chance of either 1 black and 5 white, or 5 black and 1 white; and just a 1.6% chance of either 6 blacks and no white, or 6 whites and no black.

This information about the sample results is summarised in Figure 12.2. The graph shows a sampling distribution, so called because it is the distribution of all possible sample results for a particular sample size. As in Chapter 11, the sampling distribution shows three things:

1 The distribution is centred on the actual population breakdown of black and white balls.
2 The central sample result is also the most likely sample result.
3 The distribution is symmetrical – the left-hand side of the graph is a mirror image of the right-hand side.

Variability in sample results – a real-life example

Fortunately, these general points also apply to much larger real-life studies. Imagine that you have the results of a poll asking 250 students about their voting intentions

6B, 0W	5B, 1W	4B, 2W	3B, 3W	2B, 4W	1B, 5W	0B, 6W
			BBBWWW			
			WBRRWW			
			WWBBBW			
			WWWBBB			
			BBWBWW			
		WWBBBD	BBWWBW	BBWWWW		
		BWWBBB	BBWWWB	WBBWWW		
		BBWWBB	WBBWBW	WWBBWW		
		BBBWWB	WBBWWB	WWWBBW		
		BBBBWW	WWBBWB	WWWWBB		
		WBWBBB	BWBBWW	BWBWWW		
		RWBWBB	DWWBBW	WBWBWW		
		BBWBWB	BWWWBB	WWBWBW		
		BBBWBW	WBWBBW	WWWBWB		
	WBRRRB	WBDWDB	WBWWBB	BWWBWW	BWWWWW	
	BWBBBB	RWRBWB	WWDWBB	WBWWBW	WBWWWW	
	BDWBBB	BHWBBW	BWBWBW	WWBWWB	WWBWWW	
	BBBWBB	WBBBWB	WBWBWB	BWWWBW	WWWBWW	
	BBBBWB	BWBBBW	BWWBWB	WBWWWB	WWWWBW	
BBBBBB	BBBBBW	WBBBBW	BWBWWB	BWWWWB	WWWWWB	WWWWWW

Results	6B, 0W	5B, 1W	4B, 2W	3B, 3W	2B, 4W	1B, 5W	0B, 6W
N of results	1	6	15	20	15	6	1
% of results	1.6	9.4	23.4	31.3	23.4	9.4	1.6

Figure 12.1   All possible sample results: sampling 6 balls from equal numbers of black and white balls

in an election for student president. It looks reasonably clear: 55% say they will vote for Jo, and 45% will vote for Chris. Provided the results are based on probability sampling, the best single estimate (a *point estimate*) of the population percentage is the one given by the sample. In other words, you can predict that among all 25,000 students at the university, 55% will vote for Jo, and 45% will vote for Chris. Of course, people usually interpret sample results in this basic way.

However, as Chapter 11 pointed out, to leave the analysis there ignores the fact that the sample taken is only one of a much larger number of possible samples. Although the most likely sample result is the actual population value, there is no guarantee that the result from the one sample taken is the actual population percentage.

The analysis needs to take into account this variability in sample results. With the previous very small example, it was easy to work out all the possible samples

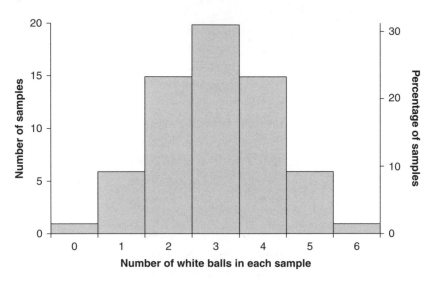

Figure 12.2   Sampling distribution: sampling 6 balls from equal numbers of black and white balls

(Figure 12.1) and draw up the sampling distribution (Figure 12.2). Things are a bit more complicated in real-life research, but the basic ideas are the same. The following paragraphs show how you can estimate the population percentage from the results of just a single sample.

When you have categorical data, you can use the sample percentage in a category to estimate the population percentage in the same category. Thus, you can use the sample survey of 250 students to say something about the voting intentions of all 25,000 students at the university.

The sample taken is only one of many millions of possible different samples of 250 from the population of 25,000. These millions of samples will show a range of results. As in Chapter 11, the distribution of all the sample percentages is normal in shape, and centred on the population percentage (i.e. the percentage you would get if you polled all 25,000 students).

As with any other distribution, you measure the variability of this sampling distribution by its standard deviation. Recall that the standard deviation of a sampling distribution is termed a *standard error*. Chapter 11 referred to 'the standard error of the mean', because the chapter deals with numerical data. Here, it's the 'standard error of the percentage' because with categorical data you're interested in measuring the percentage in a particular category. You calculate it as follows:

$$\text{Standard error of the percentage} = \sqrt{\frac{\text{Population\%} \times (100 - \text{Population\%})}{\text{Size of sample}}}$$

The 'Population %' is the percentage of individuals making up the population who are in the category that interests you (e.g. the percentage who say they'll vote for Jo). The '100 – Population %' is the remaining percentage (e.g. the percentage who say they'll vote for Chris). Obviously, these two values add up to 100. However, as with numerical data, there is a catch-22 situation here.

Yossarian, the main character in Joseph Heller's classic Second World War novel, *Catch-22*, applies for exemption from flying on the grounds that he is insane. However, trying to avoid something as dangerous as wartime flying is clearly the act of a *sane* man – and thus someone who is fit to fly. 'Yossarian was moved very deeply by the absolute simplicity of this clause of Catch-22 and let out a respectful whistle. "That's some catch, that Catch-22," he observed' (Heller 1961: 46). *Catch-22* started out as 'Catch-18'. Shortly before publication, however, the blockbuster novelist Leon Uris produced a novel entitled *Mila 18* (also about the Second World War). It was thought advisable that Heller, the first-time novelist, should be the one to blink. Heller ... 'was heartbroken. I thought 18 was the only number.' A long process of numerical agonising began (Dexter 2007). Finally, after rejecting 'Catch-11' and 'Catch-14', Heller's editor hit on 'Catch-22'. It took two weeks to persuade Heller that this was the right title.

You need to work out the standard error to estimate the population percentage, but you need the population percentage to work out the standard error – and it's the population percentage that you want to estimate! The best available estimate of the population percentage is the sample percentage, and you use this to estimate the standard error of the sampling distribution of the percentages. In the student poll, 55% of the 250 voters in the sample supported Jo. You estimate the standard error of the sampling distribution of the percentage as follows:

$$\text{Standard error of the percentage} = \sqrt{\frac{\text{Population\%} \times (100 - \text{Population\%})}{\text{Size of sample}}}$$

$$= \sqrt{\frac{55 \times (100-55)}{250}} = \sqrt{\frac{55 \times 45}{250}} = \sqrt{\frac{2475}{205}} = 3.15$$

Thus, the standard error of the percentage is 3.15. Remember that the standard error is a measure of the variability of all possible sample percentages in the sampling distribution. The sampling distribution is centred on the population percentage. Because the distribution has a *normal* shape, you know the percentage of sample results lying within specified limits. As before, 95% of sample results lie within 2 standard errors (i.e. two standard deviation units) of the population percentage. Consequently, the one sample result that is available (55) has a 95% chance of lying within two standard errors of the population percentage. As the standard error is 3.15, the one sample result has a 95% chance of lying within two lots of 3.15 of the population percentage. In other words, the one sample result has a 95% chance of lying within 6.3 (2 × 3.15) of the population percentage.

Once again, you can turn this statement around and also say that the population percentage has a 95% chance of lying within two standard errors of the sample percentage. As the sample percentage is 55 and two standard errors are 6.3, you can be 95% confident that the population percentage lies in the range of (55 – 6.3) to (55 + 6.3). In other words, you can be 95% confident that support for Jo among all student voters lies in the range of 48.7% to 61.3%. Thus, Jo will still be pleased with the poll result – it looks as if Jo will win, possibly by a large margin. But Chris would focus on the lower confidence limit (48.7%), and see that there's still a chance of winning.

You may have some nagging doubts about the statistical sleight of hand used when substituting the sample percentage for the population percentage to calculate the standard error. However, bear in mind that the sample percentage is the best single estimate of the population percentage. Moreover, the effect of any difference between sample and population percentage becomes progressively smaller as the sample size increases. This is because, as the standard error formula shows, the top line of the equation that includes the percentage values is subsequently divided by the sample size. And the final square root reduces any error even further.

Sample size and variability in sample results

This final section looks at the issue of sample size in terms of inferential statistics. The student election research uses a reasonably large sample of 250 voters. Consequently, the sampling distribution of the sample percentages has a normal shape, is centred on the population value, and has 95% of sample results lying within two standard errors of the population value.

However, the smaller the sample, the greater the possible difference between the sampling distribution and a normal distribution, and thus the less accurate will be a confidence interval based on a normal distribution. For example, Table 12.1 shows the number of times each result can occur when drawing random samples from a drum containing equal numbers of black and white balls. The first row shows that with a sample of only 1, there are only 2 possible results, either 1 black or 1 white. The next row of Table 12.1 shows that with a sample size of only 2, there are only four possible results: (i) Black + Black, (ii) Black + White, (iii) White + Black, and (iv) White + White. The distribution of sample results is clearly not a normal curve. However, as the sample size increases, the range of possible sample results also increases, so that even with a sample as small as 6, the distribution begins to look something like a normal distribution. The last row of Table 12.1 shows the data used earlier to draw Figures 12.1 and 12.2.

As Figure 12.3 shows, by the time the sample size gets to 20, the distribution of sample percentages is approximately normal if the samples are drawn from a population in which 50% of balls are white and 50% are black.

Table 12.1   All possible results using different-sized samples. Sampling from a population with 50% white and 50% black balls

Sample size	Number of white balls in sample						
	0	1	2	3	4	5	6
1	1	1					
2[1]	1	2	1				
3	1	3	3	1			
4	1	4	6	4	1		
5	1	5	10	10	5	1	
6	1	6	15	20	15	6	1

[1] For example, 1 (B+B), 2 (W+B, B+W), 1 (W+W).

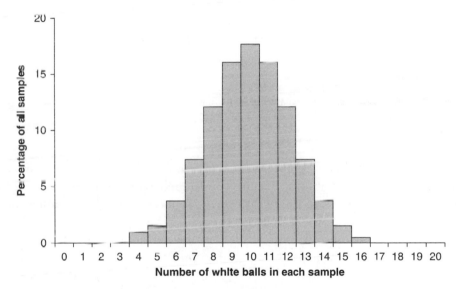

The graph is not large enough to show the small percentage of samples with less than 4 white balls or more than 16 white balls, but the same mirror-image pattern is maintained.

Figure 12.3   Sampling distribution: samples of 20 from population with 50% white and 50% black balls

However, sampling distributions of category percentages are influenced not only by the size of the sample, but also by the category percentages in the population. Notice that the caption of Figure 12.3 specifies a population with 50% white and 50% black balls. If the population breakdown were different, say 25% white and 75% black, the sampling distribution from samples of 20 balls would definitely not be normal in shape, as Figure 12.4 shows.

This pattern is not surprising when you remember that the most likely sample percentage is the population percentage. Thus, because the population includes 25% of white balls, the most commonly occurring sample result is also 25% white

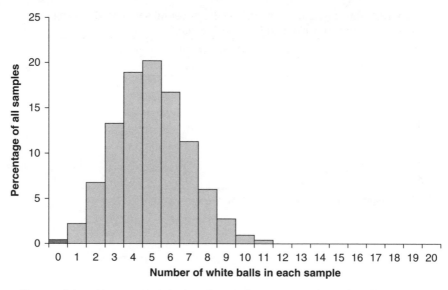

The graph is not large enough to show the small percentage of samples with 12 or more white balls, but the same pattern is maintained.

Figure 12.4   Sampling distribution: samples of 20 from population with 25% white and 75% black balls

balls (i.e. 5 white balls out of 20). As the minimum number of white balls in any sample is 0, the distribution is bunched on the left between 0 and 5, but can spread out much further on the right beyond 5. This creates a *skewed* rather than a normal distribution.

How can you factor into your calculations the percentage breakdown in the population? After all, you don't know the population percentage – indeed, it's what you are trying to estimate! Once again, you use the sample percentage as the best single estimate of the population percentage. Thus, before you can decide whether or not the sampling distribution of the percentages is normal, you need to take into account both the sample size and the sample percentage. Figure 12.3 shows that with a sample size of 20 and a sample percentage of 50, you can assume that the sampling distribution of the percentages has a normal shape. Multiplying the sample size (20) and sample percentage (50) gives a score of 1000. You can use this score of 1000 as a benchmark to decide on normality, as the following example shows.

You ask a random sample of students from your campus about whether or not they believe in astrology. The sample results show that 26% believe in astrology and 74% do not. Take the smaller of the two category percentages (26) and divide it into 1000 to show the minimum sample size necessary to allow you to assume that the sampling distribution of the percentages is normal. Dividing the category percentage of 26 into 1000 shows that the minimum number of students you need in the sample is 38. If you do not already have a sample of at least 38, you would need to increase your sample size by surveying more students. Once you have at least the minimum sample size, you calculate the standard error of the sample percentages in the usual way.

<hr>

BEHIND THE STATS

A survey of students on a large Australian first-year university science course showed that 26% believed that 'the position of the stars and planets can affect people's lives' (Bridgstock 2003: 8). An international poll by Gallup (Lyons 2005) showed that one-quarter of the general populations of the USA, Canada, and the UK believed in astrology. There was a marked difference by gender, with belief in astrology higher among women than among men (USA: 28% women, 23% men; Canada: 23% women, 17% men; UK: 30% women, 14% men).

<hr>

The next chapter continues the theme of using sample results to say something about the population from which the sample comes. However, the focus moves away from estimating means and category percentages. Instead, Chapter 13 introduces the idea of hypothesis testing, which is the underlying theme of the remaining chapters in the book.

Part Five

Hypothesis testing

THIRTEEN

Introducing hypothesis testing

Chapter Overview

This chapter will:

- Define *hypothesis testing* as the procedure to work out how likely it is that a specific prediction about the population is correct.
- Show how the first step is to develop a *null hypothesis* and an *alternative hypothesis*.
- Show how the second step is to locate the sample in the sampling distribution.
- Show how the final step is to decide whether to reject or retain the null hypothesis using a predetermined benchmark or significance level.

As well as estimating population characteristics, researchers use another major type of data analysis, called *hypothesis testing*. This chapter introduces hypothesis testing, and the following chapters look in more detail at hypothesis testing for categorical data (Chapter 14), numerical data (Chapter 15), and combinations of the two (Chapter 16).

In these chapters, a *hypothesis* is a specific, testable prediction about the population. Hypothesis testing is the procedure used to work out how likely it is that the prediction is correct. A very simple example will help to explain the basic hypothesis-testing procedure. A man in a bar claims to have powers of psychokinesis – that he can control the movement of inanimate objects with his mind. As a good researcher, you are sceptical of his claimed psychokinetic powers. You ask him for evidence to allow you to test his claim. By some incredible chance, the bar has a lottery drum containing equal numbers of black and white balls. You ask the man to use his powers to influence the movement of the balls in the drum. He agrees, and says that he will use psychokinesis to draw out balls of the same colour.

BEHIND THE STATS

The term *psi* (pronounced 'sigh') refers to two broad types of psychic or paranormal phenomena: (i) psychokinesis, which includes controlling inanimate objects and your own or other people's bodies (e.g. levitation, miraculous cures); and (ii) extra sensory perception, which includes telepathy and clairvoyance. The mainstream scientific community is generally highly critical of psi. The few high-profile supporters, such as Brian Josephson, winner of a Nobel Prize for Physics, are publicly derided (e.g. McKie 2001). The problem, of course, is the difficulty of explaining psi with current scientific thinking. For example, the Princeton Engineering Anomalies Research project found that subjects influenced results from a random event generator several days *after* the running of the machine (McCrone 1994: 37)!

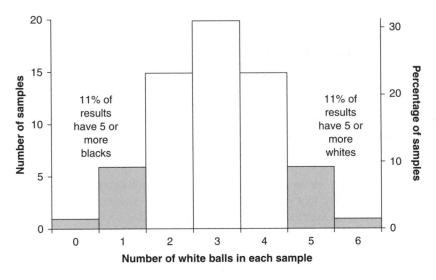

Figure 13.1   All possible sample results: sampling 6 balls from a population with equal numbers of black and white balls

In his lifetime, the man could try to influence the results from millions of rolls of the drum. This is the 'population', of which the few rolls of the drum he does with you are just a small sample. In line with your initial scepticism, your hypothesis about the population is that it will show no evidence of psychokinesis. If your hypothesis is right, your sample is from this population. Only if the sample result warrants it will you support an alternative hypothesis that the man does have psychokinetic powers.

The next step is to get a sample result. The man concentrates on the drum, you roll it, and a white ball appears. You replace it, spin the drum a second time, and another white ball appears, then a third white ball, then a fourth and a fifth white ball; however, on the sixth roll a black ball appears. The man then says that he can feel his psychokinetic powers fading for the evening, refuses to continue the experiment – and demands a large whisky from you. The sample result, therefore, is 5 white balls and 1 black ball.

You use this small set of sample data to test your hypothesis statistically. Figure 13.1 (based on Figure 12.1) shows the sampling distribution from randomly sampling 6 balls from equal numbers of black and white balls. In other words, it shows the number of black and white balls expected when the only influence on the results is chance (i.e. not psychokinesis). Overall, 11% of all results (7 of 64) have 5 or more white balls.

You then think back to what the man agreed to do – to draw out balls of the same colour. He did not specify whether they were black or white balls. Thus, if there had been 5 *black* balls in the sample rather than 5 white, he would similarly have used the result to back up his claim. Figure 13.1 also shows that there are 7 ways of getting at least 5 black balls in 6 draws – another 11% chance. Thus, without any psychokinetic ability whatsoever, the man has a 22% (11 + 11) chance of getting 5 balls of one colour in 6 draws.

You now need to make a decision about your initial hypothesis that the man does not have psychokinetic abilities. Does the result suggest that your initial scepticism might be wrong? Drawing 5 balls with the same colour from 6 draws occurs by chance alone 22% of the time. In other words, there's a better than 1 in 5 chance of this result occurring without psychokinesis. You will probably decide that this result is not unusual enough for you to abandon your initial scepticism. So you retain your hypothesis that the man has no psychokinetic abilities.

The psychokinesis example shows that there are three basic steps in hypothesis testing:

1 Make a hypothesis, or specific testable prediction, about the population.
2 Take a sample and locate it in the relevant sampling distribution.
3 Decide whether to reject or retain the hypothesis.

The following sections look more carefully at each of these steps. They use an example of research into participation in student organisations. Researchers have a hunch that there is a difference between male and female students in terms of their participation in student groups. To test this hunch, they find the gender breakdown of candidates for a sample of elections for positions on the boards of management of various student clubs and societies. The results show that of 140 candidates, 60% are women and 40% are men. University records show that 50% of students are women and 50% are men.

Make a hypothesis about the population

Always remember that a hypothesis is a specific, testable prediction about the population. In this example, the population consists of all candidates for student elections. The prediction is that there is a difference in participation rates of men and women. However, it is not this prediction that you test directly, but rather its opposite – that the sample is from a population in which there is *no* difference in the participation rates of men and women.

At first glance, this approach seems a bit bizarre. But how, for example, can you prove the hypothesis that 'All grizzly bears are brown'? Basically, you can't. No matter how long and hard you look and find only brown grizzly bears, the next could be another colour. However, it is much easier to disprove the hypothesis that 'All grizzly bears are brown'. All you need is one bear that is not brown.

You now need to translate this general prediction that there is no difference in the participation rates of men and women into a specific, testable hypothesis. Recall that you need to test the prediction that there is *no* difference in the participation rates of male and female students. If this prediction is true, you would expect 50% of all election candidates to be women. This is because university records show that 50% of all students are women. In other words, you predict that because there is no difference in the participation rates of male and female students, 50% of the population of all election candidates will be women. (Similarly, if 75% of all students were women, you would predict that women make up 75% of election candidates.) This specific, testable prediction is the *null hypothesis*, from the Latin word *nullus*, meaning 'no' or 'none'.

BEHIND THE STATS

Much of the southern part of Australia is made up of a plain called the Nullarbor, meaning 'no trees'. Edward John Eyre was the first European to cross the Nullarbor, in 1841. He wrote in his journal that the area included some of 'the wildest and most inhospitable wastes of Australia' (Eyre 1845: 2), though that could have been because his expedition was marred by supply problems, mutiny, theft, and murder (Dutton 2006). Edward *Eyre* is not to be confused with Henry *Ayers*, a local politician after whom the 335 metre (1100 feet) high sandstone rock in central Australia is named. Ayers Rock is now also known by its traditional Aboriginal name, Uluru.

What if the evidence is strong enough to allow you to reject the null hypothesis? You need an *alternative hypothesis*. The simplest and best advice is to make the alternative hypothesis the direct opposite to the null hypothesis. Thus, if the null hypothesis is that there is *no* difference, the alternative is that there *is* a difference. At this point, don't specify the *direction* of any difference (i.e. that women participate more than men, or that men participate more than women). In this example, the null hypothesis is that there is no difference in the participation rates of men and women. Thus, the alternative hypothesis is that there *is* a difference in the participation rates of men and women. If this is the case, women do not make up 50% of all student election candidates – it could be more than 50%, or it could be less than 50%.

The two hypotheses (plural of hypothesis) are thus as follows:

- *Null hypothesis* The sample comes from a population in which there is *no* difference in the participation rates of men and women: women make up 50% of all student election candidates.
- *Alternative hypothesis* The sample comes from a population in which there *is* a difference in the participation rates of men and women: women do not make up 50% of all student election candidates.

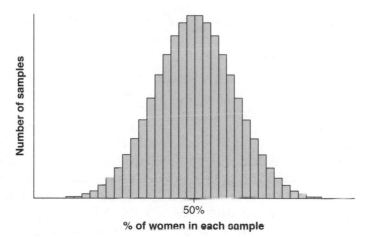

Figure 13.2 Sampling distribution if null hypothesis is true, (i.e. women make up 50% of election candidates)

Take a sample and locate it in the sampling distribution

In the sample of 140 students, 60% are women. The next stage is to compare this actual or observed sample result to the result you would expect if the null hypothesis is correct – in other words, if the sample *has* been drawn from a population with 50% women. Imagine that you draw every possible sample of 140 students from a large population with 50% women, find the percentage of women in each sample, and then graph the millions of sample percentages. Figure 13.2 shows the sampling distribution of the percentage results. Following on from the previous chapters, you would expect this sampling distribution to have a normal shape and be centred on the population percentage specified in the null hypothesis (50%).

Recall from Chapter 12 that you calculate the standard error (i.e. the standard deviation) of this sampling distribution of percentage values as follows:

$$\text{Standard error of sampling distribution of \%} = \sqrt{\frac{\text{Population \% } \times (100 - \text{Population \%})}{\text{Size of sample}}}$$

In this example, the 'Population %' is the expected percentage of women candidates in all student elections. The null hypothesis says that women make up 50% of the population. Thus, with a sample size of 140, the calculation of the standard error of the percentage (SE%) is as follows:

$$\text{SE\%} = \sqrt{\frac{\text{Population \% } \times (100 - \text{Population \%})}{\text{Size of sample}}} = \sqrt{\frac{50 \times (100 - 50)}{140}} =$$

$$\sqrt{\frac{50 \times 50}{140}} = \sqrt{17.86} = 4.23$$

Thus, the standard error of the sampling distribution of the percentage results is 4.23. Figure 13.3 shows this information on the normal curve. A sample result of 54.23 is one standard error more than the expected population percentage. This is because 54.23 is 4.23 more than 50, and each standard error is 4.23. Similarly, 58.46 is two standard errors more than the population percentage because 58.46 is 8.46, or two lots of 4.23, more than 50.

Because the sampling distribution has a normal shape, approximately 95% of all sample results lie within two standard errors of the population percentage (i.e. from the population percentage minus two standard errors to the population percentage plus two standard errors). In this example, therefore, approximately 95% of all sample results lie between 41.54 (i.e. two standard errors less than the mean) and 58.46 (i.e. two standard errors more than the mean). If 95% of the sample results lie between 41.54 and 58.46, then the remaining 5% of sample results lie outside this range. The one sample result available (i.e. 60) lies outside this range. Thus, you now know that there is less than a 5% chance of a sample of this size with 60% women being drawn from a population with 50% women. In other words, there is less than a 5% probability that the sample comes from the population specified in the null hypothesis.

You can work out more exactly the probability of your sample coming from the population specified in the null hypothesis. The first step is to measure how far away the observed sample percentage (60) is from the expected population percentage (50) in terms of the standard error (4.23). Thus, the sample percentage is 10 away from the population percentage (i.e. 60 – 50), which is the equivalent to 2.36 standard error units (i.e. 10 ÷ 4.23). The term *z-score* is often used for standard error units. Thus, the sample result (60) has a z-score of 2.36. The z-score is known as the *test statistic* – the statistic used to test the hypothesis. In more formal terms, the calculation of this z-score test statistic looks like this:

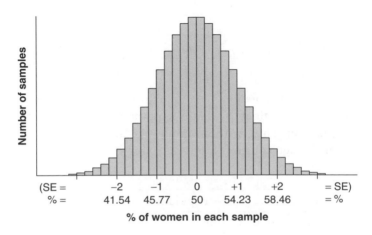

Figure 13.3   Sampling distribution with standard error values: population % = 50, standard error of sampling distribution = 4.23

$$z\text{-score} = \frac{\text{Observed sample \% } - \text{ Expected population \%}}{\text{Standard error of sampling distribution of \%}}$$

$$= \frac{60 - 50}{4.23} = \frac{10}{4.23} = 2.36$$

A z-score of 2.36 thus indicates a sample percentage that is 10 away from the hypothesised population percentage of 50. A sample percentage that is 10 *more* than the population percentage (i.e. 60) has a z-score of *plus* 2.36 (+2.36); a sample percentage that is 10 *less* than the population percentage (i.e. 40) has a z-score of *minus* 2.36 (−2.36). You are interested in both types of result because you are trying to find out simply whether there is a *difference* between women and men in terms of election participation, not specifically whether women's rate of participation is higher or lower than men's. In other words, as Figure 13.4 shows, you are interested in *both* ends (or *tails*) of the normal distribution. The right tail shows sample results which are at least 10 more than the population percentage (like the one you have); and the left tail shows sample results which are at least 10 less than the population percentage.

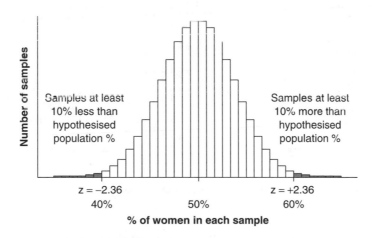

Figure 13.4   Two tails of the normal distribution

Once you have standardised the sample percentage into a z-score, you can find out more precisely the probability of a sample coming from the population specified in the null hypothesis. Figure 13.5 shows that a z-score of 1.96 cuts off the most extreme 5% of sample results, the left-hand tail of the normal distribution with the lowest 2.5% of sample results, and the right-hand tail with the highest 2.5% of sample results. (Previously, I have rounded off the 1.96 value to 2, but now is a good time to be more precise when measuring the sampling distribution.)

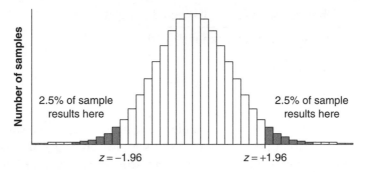

Figure 13.5   Most extreme 5% of samples in sampling distribution

Similarly, Figure 13.6 shows that a z-score of 2.33 cuts off the most extreme 2% of sample results, 1% in each of the tails. In other words, sample results which have z-scores of 2.33 or more (disregarding the sign) have, at most, only a 2% chance of coming from the population specified in the null hypothesis.

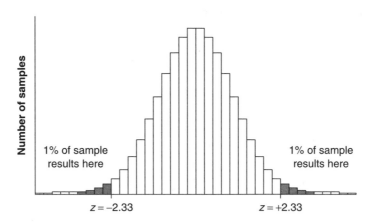

Figure 13.6   Most extreme 2% of samples in sampling distribution

Figure 13.7 shows that a z-score of 2.58 cuts off the most extreme 1% of sample results, 0.5% in each tail. In other words, sample results which have z-scores of 2.58 or more (disregarding the sign) have, at most, only a 1% chance of being drawn from the population specified in the null hypothesis.

One further result, which is not possible to show on a graph, is that a z-score of 3.29 cuts off the most extreme 0.1% of sample results, 0.05% in each tail. In other words, sample results which have z-scores of 3.29 or more (disregarding the sign) have, at most, only a 0.1% chance of being drawn from the population specified in the null hypothesis.

The values of z mentioned above (1.96, 2.33, 2.58, and 3.29) are termed *critical values*. Table 13.1 shows all these critical values.

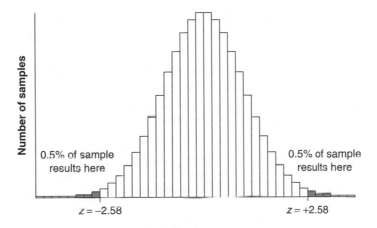

Figure 13.7   Most extreme 1% of samples in sampling distribution

Table 13.1   Critical values of z

	% of samples in two tails combined			
	5%	2%	1%	0.1%
z-value cutting off tails	1.96	2.33	2.58	3.29

The value of z in the student election research is 2.36. This z-score lies between the 2.33 and 2.58 critical values:

5%	2%	1%	0.1%
1.96	2.33	2.58	3.29
	↑		
Calculated z-score = 2.36			

Thus, when drawing a sample from the population in the null hypothesis, you can expect a sample result of 2.36 to occur less than 2% of the time (because 2.33 is less than 2.36) but more than 1% of the time (because 2.58 is more than 2.36). The results of the student election research thus show that there is less than 2 chances in 100 of a sample with 60% women coming from a population with 50% women. The sample result therefore has a *probability value* of less than 2%.

Decide whether to reject or retain the null hypothesis

You now know that there is less than a 2% probability that the sample comes from the population in the null hypothesis. Is this probability low enough for you to *reject* the null hypothesis? More statistics will not help you answer this question. Instead, you must set a probability cut-off value, and base your decision about the null hypothesis on how the sample result compares.

Lecturers use a similar procedure when deciding whether to pass or fail assignments. A common cut-off percentage is 50: those with 50% or more pass; those with less than 50% fail. Obviously, there is very little difference between an assignment with 49% and one with 50%. But a cut-off point needs to be drawn, and convention and experience suggest that 50% is about right (Figure 13.8(a)).

(a) Deciding whether to pass or fail an assignment

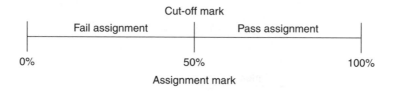

(b) Deciding whether to reject or retain a hypothesis

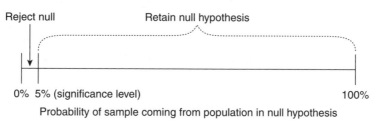

Figure 13.8 Decision-making benchmarks

In hypothesis testing in social research, the conventional cut-off point for the probability level is 5%. (It can be much less than this, 1% or lower, in medical research where decisions, literally, have life or death implications.) If the statistical test shows that the probability of a sample coming from the population specified in the null hypothesis is 5% or less, then you reject the null hypothesis. If the sampling distribution shows that a sample has more than a 5% chance of coming from the population specified in the null hypothesis, then you retain the null hypothesis. This 5% value is thus very significant – it determines your decision about what to do with the null hypothesis. That's why it's called the 5% *significance level*. In fact, testing a hypothesis is often referred to as making a *test of significance*.

Using a significance level of 5%, you reject the null hypothesis that the sample is from a population with 50% women. This is because a sample with 60% or more women occurs less than 2 times in 100 when you draw samples of 140 students from a population with 50% women. Having rejected the null hypothesis, you can now support the alternative hypothesis, and say that the sample does *not* come from a population with 50% women.

The sample shows that *more* than 50% of candidates are women, and this is what you can also expect to find in the population. As university records show that exactly half of all students are women, you can therefore predict that in the university as a whole there is a difference in election participation rates of men and women: women are *more* likely to stand for election. Table 13.2 summarises the steps taken to make this decision.

Table 13.2   Steps in hypothesis testing (e.g. student elections)

Sample (e.g. sample size = 140)	Sampling distribution (e.g. all samples of 140)	Population (all election candidates)
		1 Devise *null hypothesis*, e.g. female population is 50%
		2 Devise *alternative hypothesis*, e.g. female population is not 50%
		3 Set *significance level*, e.g. 5%
4 Calculate *test statistic*, e.g. $z = 2.36$		
	5 Find *probability value*, i.e probability of sample coming from population in null hypothesis, e.g. probability – less than 2%	
		6 Make *decision about null hypothesis*, e.g. probability value is less than 2%, significance level is 5%, so reject null hypothesis and support alternative hypothesis
		7 Make *prediction about population* from which sample is drawn, e.g. *more* women candidates than expected – women's participation rate is *higher* than men's

If you have worked your way successfully through this chapter, then you have completed most of the intellectual work needed to understand hypothesis testing. The following three chapters simply show how to apply these ideas to the various types of data you'll come across in statistical analysis. Thus, the next chapter, Chapter 14, focuses on categorical variables; Chapter 15 looks at numerical variables; and the final chapter focuses on those situations where there is both a categorical and a numerical variable.

FOURTEEN

Hypotheses about categories

Chapter Overview

This chapter will:

- Show how to test a hypothesis about one categorical variable using a *chi-square goodness-of-fit test*.
- Show how to test a hypothesis about two categorical variables using a *chi-square test for independence*.

Chapter 13 introduced the basic steps of hypothesis testing:

1   Devise a null hypothesis.
2   Devise an alternative hypothesis.
3   Set the significance level.
4   Calculate the statistical test using the sample results.
5   Find the probability level.
6   Make a decision to retain or reject null hypothesis.
7   If null hypothesis is rejected, predict the direction of the difference or association in the population.

If you have worked your way through Chapter 13, then you have done most of the hard work about hypothesis testing. This chapter and the next two simply apply the basic procedure outlined in Chapter 13 to a few of the many test statistics available for hypothesis testing. This chapter looks at how to test hypotheses about categorical variables. As Table 14.1 shows, this has two parts: (i) testing hypotheses about a single variable; and (ii) testing hypotheses about two variables.

Hypotheses about one categorical variable

The *z test of a sample percentage* is a statistical test for one categorical variable. It appeared in Chapter 13 where the example focuses on the sex or gender of candidates in student elections. Unfortunately, this z test is limited to variables with only two categories (e.g. Sex: Men and Women). Often, of course, research is

Table 14.1   Some statistics for hypothesis testing

Variables	Statistical test
1 categorical	**z test of sample % (if there are just two categories)**
	Chi-square goodness-of-fit test (for any number of categories)
2 categorical	**Chi-square test for independence**
1 numerical	Student's one-sample t test
	Student's paired t test
2 numerical	Pearson's correlation coefficient
1 categorical +	Student's unpaired t test
1 numerical	One-way analysis of variance

based on variables with more than two categories (e.g. Marital status: Married, Single, Divorced, Separated, and Widowed). It's always possible to collapse these into just two categories (e.g. Married and Not married) but to do so means losing information. It's much better to use a test that can handle as many categories as the information provides. The chi-square goodness-of-fit test does this.

Chi-square goodness-of-fit test

The goodness-of-fit test was devised by British statistician Karl Pearson, of *Pearson's r* fame. In case you're wondering, *chi* is a letter in the Greek alphabet, and pronounced in the same way as the start of *Kylie*. The reason for the *square* part of the title will become obvious as you work through the following example.

BEHIND THE STATS

The Romans used the ancient Greek alphabet as the basis of their 23-letter Latin alphabet. This, in turn, is the basis of the English alphabet. The most recent letters in the current 26-letter English alphabet are *W,V,* and *J*. The letter W first appeared in the eleventh century. Although it is shaped as two Vs, its name 'double *U*' reflects the fact that when it was introduced *U* and *V* were interchangeable. It was not until the late seventeenth century that the current distinction between *U* and *V* became standard. Thus, the Geneva Bible of 1560 begins: 'In the beginning God created the heauen and the earth.' A similar history also applies to *I* and *J*. The distinction between these two letters was not completely resolved until the early nineteenth century. The most used letter in English is *E*, and the least used is *Q*. See David Crystal's fascinating *Cambridge Encyclopedia of the English Language* (2003).

Being known for your statistical insights, you are asked to settle a dispute about whether or not a student has been gambling with a loaded dice. The general opinion is that the dice is loaded – which is strenuously denied by the alleged cheat. You start with the idea that the dice is fair. You will reject this point of view only if the evidence is strong. After all, you don't want to convict an innocent person.

If the dice is fair, each of the six sides will have an equal chance of turning up. Thus, if you throw a fair dice 60 times, you expect each side to turn up 10 times:

Dice side	1	2	3	4	5	6
Number of times expected	10	10	10	10	10	10

These are the *expected frequencies*. To produce some sample data to work on, you roll the suspect dice 60 times and observe the following results:

Dice side	one	two	three	four	five	six
Number of times observed	8	6	9	9	7	21

These are the *observed frequencies*. The greater the difference between the observed frequencies and the expected frequencies, the less likely it is that the suspect dice is a fair one. Side 6 turned up 21 times compared to the expected 10 times. The result certainly does not look good for the protesting dice owner. But how likely is it that such an observed set of results could be produced by a fair dice? The chi-square test will tell you.

The chi-square test works by comparing the observed frequencies (8, 6, 9, 9, 7, 21) with the expected frequencies (10, 10, 10, 10, 10, 10). The smaller the difference between the two, the smaller the chi-square value. If there is absolutely *no* difference between the observed and expected frequencies, the chi-square result is 0. If the null hypothesis is true and the dice *is* a fair one, you would expect the observed and expected frequencies to be very similar, and the chi-square result to be close to 0.

The procedure for calculating chi-square is as follows:

$$\text{Chi-square} = \text{Sum of} \left(\frac{(\text{Each observed frequency} - \text{Each associated expected frequency})^2}{\text{Each associated expected frequency}} \right)$$

For example, the top row of Table 14.2 shows that side 1 turned up 8 times, but was expected to turn up 10 times. Thus, its observed frequency is 8, and its expected frequency is 10. The difference between the observed and expected frequencies is − 2 (8 − 10), which when squared becomes 4 (−2 × −2). Each of the difference squared values (e.g. 4) is then divided by the expected value (10) to produce a standardised result (e.g. 4 ÷ 10 = 0.40). You do the same calculations for each of the remaining five dice sides, and then add the six individual results to produce an overall chi-square statistic. Table 14.2 shows all the calculations. The chi-square result is 15.20.

Table 14.2   Chi-square calculation: 'loaded' dice example

Categories (dice side)	Frequencies		$O - E$	$(O - E)^2$	$(O - E)^2 \div E$
	Observed	Expected			
1	8	10	$8 - 10 = -2$	$-2 \times -2 = 4$	$4 \div 10 = 0.40$
2	6	10	$6 - 10 = -4$	$-4 \times -4 = 16$	$16 \div 10 = 1.60$
3	9	10	$9 - 10 = -1$	$-1 \times -1 = 1$	$1 \div 10 = 0.10$
4	9	10	$9 - 10 = -1$	$-1 \times -1 = 1$	$1 \div 10 = 0.10$
5	7	10	$7 - 10 = -3$	$-3 \times -3 = 9$	$9 \div 10 = 0.90$
6	21	10	$21 - 10 = 11$	$11 \times 11 = 121$	$121 \div 10 = 12.10$
Total	**60**	**60**			**Chi-square = 15.20**

What is the probability (i.e. chance) of drawing a sample with a chi-square result of at least 15.20 with a fair dice? To answer this question, you locate the sample result in the relevant sampling distribution. Imagine that you throw a fair dice 60 times, note the number of times that each side appears, and calculate chi-square from these observed frequencies. You then repeat the process a billion more times, and graph the billion and one chi-square results. Figure 14.1 shows the resulting sampling distribution.

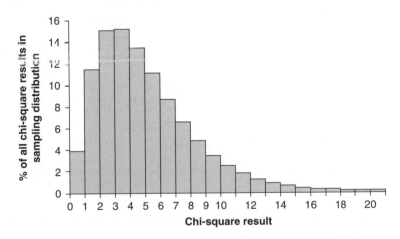

Figure 14.1   Sampling distribution of chi-square: one variable with six categories

Figure 14.1 shows that about 4% of chi-square results are less than 1, about 11% are between 1 and 1.99, almost 15% are between 2 and 2.99, and just over 15% are between 3 and 3.99. Then there is an ever-declining percentage of results in each bar as the chi-square values get larger, so that by the time chi-square reaches 14, each bar contains less than 1% of the total number of results.

You expect fewer high chi-square values than low ones. This is because, with a fair dice, each side should generally turn up about the same number of times, and thus be very little different from the null hypothesis frequencies of 10 per side. Consequently, the chi-square value will be low. At first glance, it's a bit surprising that the tallest bar is not the one on the left, representing chi-square values of less than 1. However, the shape of the distribution makes sense when you think about an example in which you throw a fair dice 60 times, and find that after 59 throws there are 10 ones, 10 twos, 10 threes, 10 fours, 10 fives, and 9 sixes. On the 60th throw, there is only 1 chance in 6 that side 6 will turn up, but 5 chances in 6 that one of the other sides will appear. In other words, a slightly uneven result (e.g. 10, 10, 10, 10, 11, 9) is five times more likely than an exactly even result (i.e. 10, 10, 10, 10, 10, 10).

Figure 14.2 shows information about the probability of chi-square values occurring. It shows that in the sampling distribution 5% of sample results are at least 11.07, 2% are at least 13.39, 1% are at least 15.09, and only 0.1% of chi-square results are at least 20.52. Table 14.3 also shows these critical values.

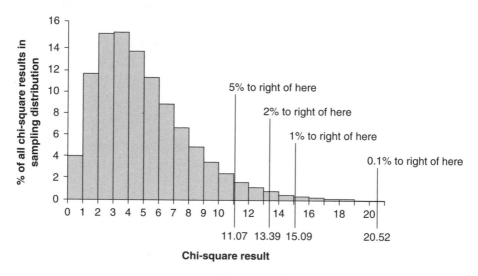

Figure 14.2   Critical values of sampling distribution of chi-square: one variable with six categories

Table 14.3   Critical values of sampling distribution of chi-square: one variable with six categories

Probability level	5%	2%	1%	0.1%
Critical value	11.07	13.39	15.09	20.52
			↑	
			Calculated chi-square = 15.20	

Table 14.3 also shows that the calculated chi-square result from the suspect dice data is 15.20, which comes between the 15.09 and 20.52 critical values. Thus, there is less than a 1% probability of a fair dice producing results with a chi-square score of at least 15.20. This means that you can reject the null hypothesis,

and support the alternative hypothesis that the dice is loaded. Table 14.4 summarises the hypothesis testing about the suspect dice.

Table 14.4   Hypothesis testing using chi-square goodness of fit: suspect dice example

Step	'Loaded' dice result
1 Devise null hypothesis	Sample comes from a population in which there is no difference in the frequency that each dice side turns up (i.e. dice not loaded). In 60 throws, each side turns up 10 times
2 Devise alternative hypothesis	Sample comes from a population in which there is a difference in the frequency that each dice side turns up (i.e. dice is loaded). In 60 throws, each side does not turn up 10 times
3 Set significance level	5%
4 Calculate test statistic	One categorical variable with six categories: chi-square goodness-of-fit test = 15.20
5 Find probability level	Probability value is less than 1%
6 Make decision about null hypothesis	Significance level is 5% Probability value is less than 1% Reject null and accept alternative hypothesis
7 Make prediction about population	There is a difference in the frequency that each dice side turns up. Side 6 turns up most often in the sample. Also likely to occur in the population

BEHIND THE STATS

The word *dice* shows how the English language can change quite quickly over time. Today, *dice* is used as both a singular and plural noun (e.g. one dice, two dice). Traditionally, the singular of *dice* was *die*. But *die* is now found almost exclusively in the phrase 'The die is cast', meaning 'the decision has been made and can't be changed'. Other nouns with non-standard plurals which are undergoing similar changes include *agendum/agenda*, *datum/data*, and possibly *criterion/criteria* and *phenomenon/phenomena*. More generally, aspects of writing that we now see almost as 'natural' have not always been part of the written language. For example, lower case letters were not introduced into English until the Middle Ages. In ancient Greece, writing was even more complex. In addition to all letters being in capitals, there were no gaps between words. Lines of text started alternately on the left and then on the right, with words on lines starting on the right being a *mirror image* of those on lines starting on the left (Ogg 1963: 89)! Thus, some lines in ancient Greek writing looked like this:

SOMELINESINANCIENTGREEKWRITINGLOOKEDLIKETHIS

The sampling distribution and associated critical values shown in Figure 14.2 and Table 14.3 apply only when the chi-square calculation is based on a single variable with six categories. As Figure 14.3 shows, the exact shape of the sampling distribution of chi-square varies with the number of categories used in the calculation.

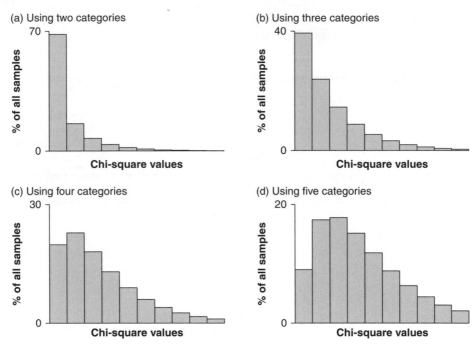

Figure 14.3 Sampling distributions of chi-square

Fortunately, statisticians have worked out the exact shape of each sampling distribution. Consequently, software packages such as SPSS and Minitab give you not only the chi-square result, but also the probability of drawing the sample from the population in the null hypothesis. For example, the printout of results from the dice experiment might look like this:

N = 60, DF = 5, Chi-Sq = 15.2, P-value = 0.01

Two of the four values are clear from the previous calculations: 'N = 60' refers to the 60 throws of the dice; and 'Chi-Sq = 15.2' is the chi-square result shown above. The other two need more explanation.

The reference to 'DF = 5' refers to the sampling distribution used in the hypothesis testing. DF is shorthand for Degrees of Freedom. It describes the 'freedom' you have to put frequency values into a table where the totals are given. For example, as Figure 14.4 shows, in the dice example there are six categories which have a total frequency of 60. You have the 'freedom' to put values into five of the boxes, but the value in the sixth box is then fixed by the pre-set total. For example, you are free to put 8 in the first box, 6 in the second box, 9 in the third, 9 in the fourth, and 7 in the fifth; but then the value of the sixth box is fixed at 21 because all six boxes have to add up to 60. Thus, there are 5 degrees of freedom. In a chi-square goodness-of-fit test, the number of degrees of freedom is always one less than the number of categories.

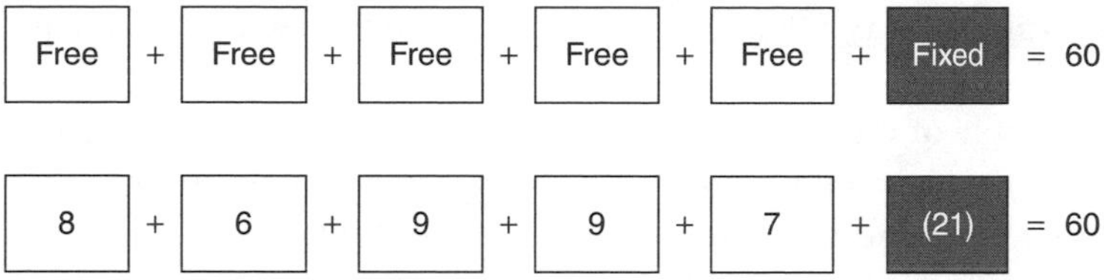

| Free | + | Free | + | Free | + | Free | + | Free | + | Fixed | = 60 |

| 8 | + | 6 | + | 9 | + | 9 | + | 7 | + | (21) | = 60 |

Figure 14.4   Logic behind degrees of freedom

The use of degrees of freedom goes back to when researchers calculated test statistics by hand, and found the probability level of the test result by looking at a table of critical values such as Table 14.5. Because the same table was often used for more than one version of a statistical test, researchers identified the correct set of critical values using degrees of freedom. The note to Table 14.5 shows this. For example, the correct number of degrees of freedom with a chi-square goodness-of-fit test is one less than the number of categories. Thus, with six categories there are 5 degrees of freedom. This row of the table shows the critical values for the sampling distribution needed to test the sample result. Once again, you can see that a chi-square result of 15.20 occurs less than 1% of the time when drawing a sample from the population specified in the null hypothesis.

Table 14.5   Critical values of chi-square

Degrees of freedom[1]	Probability level			
	5%	2%	1%	0.1%
1	3.84	5.41	6.64	10.83
2	5.99	7.82	9.21	13.82
3	7.82	9.84	11.34	16.27
4	9.49	11.67	13.28	18.46
5	11.07	13.39	15.09	20.52
6	12.59	15.03	16.81	22.46
7	14.07	16.62	19.48	24.32
8	15.51	18.17	20.09	26.12
9	16.92	19.68	21.67	27.88
10	18.31	21.16	23.21	29.59

[1] **How many degrees of freedom to use?**

One-variable goodness-of-fit test: number of categories − 1.
Two-variable test for independence: (Number of IV categories − 1) × (Number of DV categories − 1).

The software printout also shows this probability, but in a slightly different form: 'P-value = 0.01'. The P symbol stands for *probability*, but rather than expressing it in percentage terms (i.e. as 1%), it more correctly uses a probability value. As Chapter 5 pointed out, while percentages use a 'per 100' system, proportions use a 'per 1' system of standardising. Thus, 100% is the equivalent of a proportion value of 1.0, 50% is the equivalent of 0.5, and 1% is the equivalent of 0.01. Now that the computer software gives the exact probability, you don't need to consult a table of critical values. Thus, in the case of chi-square, the degrees of freedom (DF) value could be replaced on the printout by the number of categories. However, as the DF value is shown, it's useful to know what it means.

Finally, when using chi-square bear in mind the following technical points. They are often referred to as the *assumptions* of chi-square.

First, use only frequencies, not percentages. The maximum possible value of chi-square is always equal to the total frequency. Thus, in the dice example, with a total of 60 throws, the maximum possible chi-square value is 60. However, if you use percentages, the total is 100, and thus the maximum possible chi-square also is 100. Using percentages, the calculated chi-square is a massive 25.33, greatly overestimating the true figure of 15.20. If the total number of individuals in the sample is less than 100, then a chi-square calculation based on percentages will give a value that is larger than the true chi-square value, and you may end up rejecting the null hypothesis when in fact you should retain it. If the total number of individuals in the sample is more than 100, then a chi-square calculation based on percentages will give a value that is smaller than the true chi-square value, and you may end up retaining the null hypothesis when in fact you should reject it.

Second, an individual cannot be included in more than one category. For example, you ask respondents to say whether they support or oppose nuclear power. One person says: 'On the one hand, I support it because … But on the other hand, I oppose it because …' You cannot place this person in *both* the Oppose and Support categories. You either create a new category (e.g. Support/Oppose/In two minds), or leave this respondent out of the analysis. This assumption is known as the *independence of observations*.

Third, some simple, if conservative, advice is to use chi-square only if each of the *expected* frequencies is 5 or more. This is because the test assumes that the sampling distribution of the frequencies of any *category* will be normal in shape and centred on the expected frequency. This assumption of normality does not necessarily apply when an expected frequency is very small. When an expected frequency is near to zero, the centre of the distribution is also near to zero. You cannot have *negative* frequencies, and so the sampling distribution is likely to be skewed towards the high values rather than being normal in shape. This is because there is little scope for frequencies in the sampling distribution that are less than expected, but plenty of scope for frequencies that are more than expected. In the dice example, with six categories the minimum sample size is 30 (i.e. 5 throws for each of the 6 dice sides) so a sample size of 60 is fine.

Hypotheses about two categorical variables

There are several versions of the chi-square test. You can use the *chi-square test for independence* to test a hypothesis about an association between two categorical variables with any number of categories. For example, imagine that you are enrolled at a multi-campus university where there is to be an election for president of the Student Association. There are three candidates:

- Wes, who studies at the West campus.
- Chris, who studies at the Central campus.
- Emily, who studies at the East campus.

Table 14.6 shows the results of a survey of 100 voters. The first column of figures shows that 17 of 20 voters from the West campus prefer Wes. The next column shows that 20 of 30 students from the Central campus prefer Chris. And the next column shows that 32 of 50 students from the East campus prefer Emily.

Table 14.6 Observed frequencies: student voters, by preferred candidate and campus

Preferred candidate	Campus of voter			
	West	Central	East	Total
Wes	17	8	15	40
Chris	2	20	3	25
Emily	1	2	32	35
Total	20	30	50	100

Source: Hypothetical

You thus know two characteristics about each student: (i) the campus where he or she studies (*Campus of voter*); and (ii) his or her preferred candidate in the forthcoming election (*Preferred candidate*). The independent variable is the campus of study, and the dependent variable is the preferred candidate. You are interested in finding out if in the population of all voters there is an association between these two variables. If there is, then knowing the campus of each student will help improve your prediction of the preferred candidate.

Both are categorical variables, the measured values being words not numbers (West/Central/East and Wes/Chris/Emily). When you have categorical variables, you can usefully rephrase the research question from 'Is there an *association* between the variables?' to 'Is there a *difference* between the categories?' The differences are always between the independent variable categories in terms of the dependent variable. Thus, you can rephrase the research question from 'Is there an association between the two variables?' (Preferred candidate and Campus of voter) to 'Is there a difference between the campuses in terms of the preferred candidates?'

The null hypothesis says that there is *no* difference in the voting patterns between campuses. What would the data look like if this were the case? The final column of Table 14.6 shows that 40% of *all* respondents (40 out of 100) prefer Wes. If there were no difference in the level of support for each of the candidates across the three campuses, you would expect:

- 40% of the 20 students from the Western campus to prefer Wes.
- 40% of the 30 students from the Central campus to prefer Wes.
- 40% of the 50 students from the Eastern campus to prefer Wes.

Thus, from the 20 students surveyed on the West campus, you expect 8 (i.e. 40% of 20) to prefer Wes; of the 30 students surveyed on the Central campus, you expect 12 (i.e. 40% of 30) to prefer Wes; and of the 50 students on the East campus, you expect 20 (i.e. 40% of 50) to prefer Wes.

Similarly, because 25% of *all* respondents prefer Chris, you would expect 25% of the respondents on each campus to prefer Chris. And because 35% of *all* respondents prefer Emily, you would expect 35% of the respondents on each campus to prefer Emily. Table 14.7 shows all the expected frequencies.

Table 14.7   Expected frequencies: Student voters, by preferred candidate and campus

Preferred candidate	Campus of voter			Total
	West	Central	East	
Wes	40% of 20 = 8.0	40% of 30 = 12.0	40% of 50 = 20.0	**40**
Chris	25% of 20 = 5.0	25% of 30 = 7.5	25% of 50 = 12.5	**25**
Emily	35% of 20 = 7.0	35% of 30 = 10.5	35% of 50 = 17.5	**35**
Total	**20.0**	**30.0**	**50.0**	**100**

You now enter the observed and expected frequencies into the chi-square formula, which is identical to that in the previous section:

$$\text{Chi-square} = \text{Sum of} \left(\frac{(\text{Each observed frequency} - \text{Each associated expected frequency})^2}{\text{Each associated expected frequency}} \right)$$

For example, 17 of the 20 respondents from the West campus are observed to prefer Wes. If there were no difference in voting patterns between the campuses, only 8 respondents (40% of the 20) would be expected to prefer Wes. Thus, the observed frequency for this cell is 17, and the expected frequency is 8. The chi-square value for the cell is thus:

$$\frac{(\text{Observed frequency} - \text{Associated expected frequency})^2}{\text{Associated expected frequency}} = \frac{(17-8)^2}{8}$$

$$= \frac{81}{8} = 10.13$$

Table 14.8 shows this and the rest of the chi-square calculations. The total chi-square value is 66.59.

Table 14.8   Chi-square values: student voters, by preferred candidate and campus

Preferred candidate	Campus of voter			Total
	West	Central	East	
Wes	$\dfrac{(17-8)^2}{8} = 10.13$	$\dfrac{(8-12)^2}{12} = 1.33$	$\dfrac{(15-20)^2}{20} = 1.25$	12.71
Chris	$\dfrac{(2-5)^2}{5} = 1.80$	$\dfrac{(20-7.5)^2}{7.5} = 20.83$	$\dfrac{(3-12.5)^2}{12.5} = 7.22$	29.85
Emily	$\dfrac{(1-7)^2}{7} - 5.14$	$\dfrac{(2-10.5)^2}{10.5} - 6.88$	$\dfrac{(32-17.5)^2}{17.5} = 12.01$	24.03
Total	**17.07**	**29.04**	**20.48**	**66.59**

You now locate the calculated value of chi-square (66.59) on the relevant sampling distribution. Figure 14.5 shows this, along with the critical values at the 5%, 2%, 1%, and 0.1% probability levels.

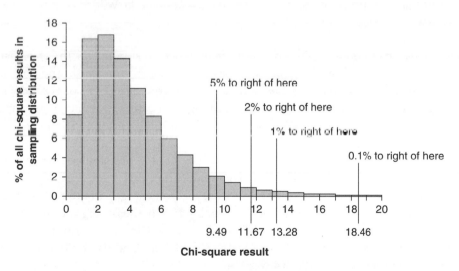

Figure 14.5   Sampling distribution and critical values of chi-square: two variables, each with three categories

The calculated chi-square value (66.59) is larger than the critical value at the 0.1% probability level (18.46):

Probability level	5%	2%	1%	0.1%
Critical value	9.49	11.67	13.28	18.46

...↑

Calculated chi-square = 66.59

Table 14.5 also showed these same critical values. You identify the correct row using the degrees of freedom advice shown in the note to the table. The reasoning behind the number of degrees of freedom is the same as explained in the previous section.

Thus, with a calculated chi-square result of 66.59 and a 0.1% critical value of 18.46, you reject the null hypothesis at the 0.1% probability level. You support the alternative hypothesis that the sample comes from a population in which there is a difference in the voting patterns across the three campuses. Expressed another way, this means that there is an association between the two variables: (i) Campus of voter; and (ii) Preferred candidate.

Table 14.8 shows that of the nine values making up chi-square, the three largest are as follows:

- *20.83* Showing the preference of voters on the Central campus for Chris, the candidate from the Central campus.
- *12.01* Showing the preference of voters on the East campus for Emily, the candidate from the East campus.
- *10.13* Showing the preference of voters on the West campus for Wes, the candidate from the West campus.

Thus, students in the sample show more than expected support for the candidate from their own campus, and you can expect this pattern to occur in the population. This difference between the campuses is also the 'direction' of the association. Much of the time, of course, when dealing with categorical data, you cannot specify any direction in an association because the categories used in the analysis have no built-in order.

You reject the null hypothesis with less than a 0.1% probability that you are doing the wrong thing. This gives you some indication that there is quite a strong association between the two variables. However, you can get a better idea of the strength of the association in the population by *directly* measuring the strength of the association in the sample. As Chapter 8 showed, lambda is a suitable coefficient of association with two categorical variables. The lambda coefficient of the observed frequencies in Table 14.6 is 0.48:

$$\text{Lambda} = \frac{\text{Sum of largest frequencies in each column} - \text{Largest row total}}{\text{Total number of individual} - \text{Largest row total}}$$

$$= \frac{(17 + 20 + 32) - 40}{100 - 40} = \frac{29}{60} = 0.48$$

This shows that knowledge of the campus of each voter leads to a 48% reduction in error when predicting the preferred candidate. In other words, there is a strong association in the sample between the two variables: (i) Campus of the voter; and (ii) Preferred candidate. The chi-square result suggests that a similar association

Table 14.9 Hypothesis testing using chi-square test for independence: student voting preferences

Step		Result
1	Devise null hypothesis	Sample comes from a population in which there is no difference in the voting patterns of students across campuses. On each campus, 40% vote for Wes, 35% vote for Emily, and 25% vote for Chris
2	Devise alternative hypothesis	Sample comes from a population in which there is a difference in the voting patterns of students across campuses
3	Set significance level	5%
4	Calculate test statistic	Two categorical variables: chi-square test for Independence = 66.59
5	Find probability level	Probability value is less than 0.1%
6	Make decision about null hypothesis	Significance level is 5% Probability value is less than 0.1% Reject null hypothesis and accept alternative hypothesis
7	Make prediction about population	Sample comes from a population in which there is a difference in the voting patterns of students across campuses. Students in the sample were more likely to vote for the candidate from their own campus. It is likely that this also occurs in the population. The lambda coefficient of 0.48 shows that there is a strong association between the two variables (Preferred candidate and Campus of voter). This supports the decision to accept the alternative

occurs in the population. Table 14.9 summarises the hypothesis-testing procedure using the student voting preference data.

Finally, bear in mind that the assumptions underlying the one-variable goodness-of-fit chi-square test also apply to a two-variable chi-square test for independence:

- Use only absolute frequencies (not percentages) in the calculation.
- Make sure that each individual is included in only one category.
- Check that all expected frequencies are at least 5.

This chapter has focused on testing hypotheses about categorical variables. The next chapter looks at exactly the same basic ideas, but shows how to work through the statistical tests that are appropriate for numerical variables.

FIFTEEN

Hypotheses about numbers

| **Chapter Overview** |

This chapter will:

- Show how to test a hypothesis about one numerical variable using a *Student's t test.*
- Show how to test a hypothesis about two numerical variables using *Pearson's correlation coefficient.*

Hypothesis testing should be quite familiar to you by now. Chapter 13 introduced the basic idea of working out the probability of a sample coming from the population described in the null hypothesis. Chapter 14 applied this to analysing categorical variables. This chapter focuses on testing hypotheses about numerical variables. The first part of the chapter looks at testing hypotheses about a single numerical variable, and the second part looks at testing hypotheses about the association between two numerical variables. Table 15.1 shows the tests covered in this chapter and in the previous and following chapters.

Table 15.1   Some statistics for hypothesis testing

Variables	Statistical test
1 categorical	z test of sample %
	Chi-square goodness-of-fit test
2 categorical	Chi-square test for independence
1 numerical	**Student's one-sample t test**
	Student's paired t test (after original two variables are combined and new variable is difference value between each pair)
2 numerical	**Pearson's correlation coefficient**
1 categorical + 1 numerical	Student's unpaired t test
	One-way analysis of variance

Hypotheses about one numerical variable – Student's *t*

This section looks at two versions of Student's *t* test: the *paired t* test; and the very similar *one-sample t* test. Chapter 11 referred to Student's *t* test, focusing on the central part of the sampling distribution. This chapter uses the same calculations and same distributions, but the focus is on the two ends (or *tails*) of the sampling distribution.

Student's paired *t* test

To illustrate Student's paired *t* test, I'll use the following example. A lecturer feels that students who cannot touch type spend so much time actually typing the first draft of their assignments that they have very little time to revise their work, and thus improve their assignment marks. In an attempt to improve matters, she pilots a small intensive touch-typing course using a random sample of 10 students from the 600 students enrolled on her course. To find out if it has been effective, she compares each student's mark for the assignment completed just before the typing course and the assignment completed just after the typing course.

BEHIND THE STATS

Technology has changed a lot in the last 135 years or so, but not the familiar QWERTY keyboard, which was patented in 1874. One explanation of the arrangement of the keys is that it slowed down typing, and thus reduced the number of times the bars carrying the keys became tangled. There are other keyboard layouts that are claimed to be more efficient. However, QWERTY has remained by far the most widely used keyboard, in part because of the major disruption that would result from any change. A minor planet is called *Qwerty*, after the keyboard layout. Astronomers now find minor planets (or *asteroids*) so often that they are discouraged from naming them after their pets, commercial products, or politicians who have not been dead for at least a century – but not keyboard layouts (CSBN 2007). The names of nearly 15,000 minor planets range alphabetically from Aakashshah to Zyskin (MPC 2009). Go to the MPC website to see if you have a minor planet named after you. (The nearest I get are the minor planets Niels and Burdett.)

What's important is the *difference* between each pair of marks. For example, Sam's score is 60 for the first assignment and 67 for the second, a difference of +7. The lecturer analyses the 10 difference scores in the sample, and finds that the assignments done after the typing course have a mean that is 6 marks higher than the mean of the earlier assignments. Thus, there is a mean difference in marks of +6.0. Further analysis shows that the standard deviation of the difference in marks is 4.0. Table 15.2 shows the results from the pilot study.

The null hypothesis is based on the idea that the typing course has no overall effect – that if all students did the typing course, the mean of the difference in

Table 15.2   Students in typing programme: assignment results

Student	Assignment 1 mark	Assignment 2 mark	Difference in marks
A	60	63	+3
B	52	61	+9
C	70	75	+5
D	60	67	+7
E	54	65	+11
F	50	48	−2
G	84	86	+2
H	66	72	+6
I	59	66	+7
J	52	64	+12

Mean of Difference in marks = 6.0

Standard deviation of Difference in marks = 4.0

Source: Hypothetical

assignment marks would be 0. The alternative hypothesis is that the typing course does have an effect – that if all students did the typing course, the mean of the difference in assignment marks would not be 0.

The hypothesis-testing procedure is the same as in the previous chapter. First, you use the sample data to calculate the test statistic. This sample of 10 students is one of millions of different samples of 10 students that you can draw from the population of all 600 students enrolled on the course. Plotting the means from all these samples creates a sampling distribution. The sampling distribution is based on the idea that the null hypothesis is correct – in this example, that there is no overall difference between the marks for the assignment completed before the touch-typing course and the marks for the assignment completed after the touch-typing course. The aim is to locate the mean result from the one sample taken in the sampling distribution, and find the probability of the sample coming from the population specified by the null hypothesis.

You use the three basic bits of information that you have about the sample:

1 Sample size (10)
2 Sample mean (+6.0)
3 Sample standard deviation (4.0).

First, you estimate the standard deviation of the population from the standard deviation of the sample (4.0) and the size of the sample (10):

$$\text{SD of population} = \text{SD of sample} \times \sqrt{\frac{\text{Size of sample}}{\text{Size of sample} -1}}$$

$$= 4 \times \sqrt{\frac{10}{9}} = 4.22$$

Then, you estimate the standard error of the sampling distribution from the standard deviation of the population (4.22) and the size of the sample (10):

$$\text{Standard error of sampling distribution} = \frac{\text{Standard deviation of population}}{\sqrt{\text{Size of sample}}}$$

$$= \frac{4.22}{\sqrt{10}} = 1.33$$

Finally, you find the position of the one sample taken in the sampling distribution that applies if the null hypothesis is correct. Recall that the null hypothesis says that the expected population mean is 0, because the typing course has no overall effect. If the null hypothesis is correct, the sampling distribution of sample means should be centred on 0. But the one sample taken has a mean of 6.0. You need to standardise this into a Student's t-score, which is simply how many standard errors the sample is away from the centre of the sampling distribution. The sample mean is 6.0 and the estimated standard error of the sampling distribution is 1.33. Thus, the sample is 4.51 standard errors away from the centre of the sampling distribution (6.0 ÷ 1.33 = 4.51). In other words, the Student's t-score is 4.51:

$$\text{Student's } t\text{-score} = \frac{\text{Observed sample mean} - \text{Expected population mean}}{\text{Standard error of sampling distribution of means}}$$

$$= \frac{6 - 0}{1.33} = 4.51$$

You can now locate a Student's t-score of 4.51 on the relevant sampling distribution. As with chi-square, there is a slightly different sampling distribution for each sample size. Figure 15.1 shows the sampling distribution for a sample with 10 individuals, along with the critical value at the 5% probability level, which is 2.26. In other words, the two t-scores −2.26 and +2.26 together cut off the extreme 5% of sample results in the sampling distribution.

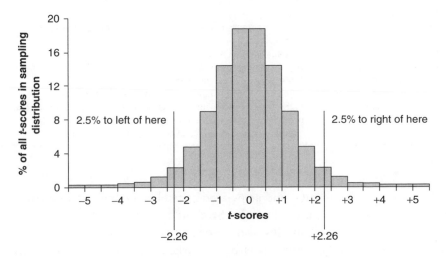

Figure 15.1   Sampling distribution of Student's t: one variable with 10 values

Table 15.3 shows several critical values for the sampling distribution in Figure 15.1. The calculated t-score (4.51) is larger than the critical value at the 1% probability level (3.25) but smaller than the critical value at the 0.1% probability level (4.78).

Table 15.3 Critical values of Student's paired t test: one variable with 10 values

Probability level	5%	2%	1%	0.1%
Critical value	2.26	2.82	3.25	4.78
			↑	
			Calculated value of $t = 4.51$	

Therefore, you reject the null hypothesis at the 1% probability level, and support the alternative hypothesis: the sample comes from a population in which there is a difference in the assignment marks. The sample result shows an *increase* in assignment marks, and this is what you would expect to happen if all students who cannot touch type did the intensive typing course. Table 15.4 summarises the hypothesis-testing example using Student's paired t test.

Table 15.4 Hypothesis testing using Student's paired t test

Step	Typing course result
1 Devise null hypothesis	Sample comes from a population in which overall there is no difference in the scores of each student's assignment done before the typing course and the assignment done after the typing course. The mean difference in these scores is 0
2 Devise alternative hypothesis	Sample comes from a population in which overall there is a difference in the scores of each student's assignment done before the typing course and the assignment done after the typing course. The mean difference in these scores is not 0
3 Set significance level	5%
4 Calculate test statistic	One numerical variable with a sample size of 10: Student's paired t test = 4.51
5 Find probability level	Probability value is less than 1%
6 Make decision about null hypothesis	Significance level is 5% Probability value is less than 1% Reject null hypothesis and accept alternative hypothesis
7 Make prediction about population	In the sample, scores for the assignment done after the typing course overall are *higher* than those for the assignment done before the typing course. This is also likely to occur in the population

The sampling distribution and associated critical values shown in Figure 15.1 and Table 15.3 apply only when the Student's paired t calculation is based on a sample size of 10. Samples of different sizes have different sampling distributions. Fortunately, statisticians have worked out the exact shape of the sampling distribution for all sample sizes. Consequently, software packages such as SPSS and Minitab give you not only the Student's t result, but also the probability of drawing the sample from the population in the null hypothesis. For example, the printout of results from the touch-typing research may include the following:

T-Test of mean difference = 0, T-Value = 4.51, P-Value = 0.002, DF = 9

1. *T-Test of mean difference = 0* This refers to the null hypothesis that the mean of the differences in the scores of each student's assignment done before the typing course and the assignment done after the typing course is 0.
2. *T-Value = 4.51* This is the calculated t test statistic of 4.51.
3. *P-Value = 0.002* This is the probability value. It's shown as a proportion (0.002). If 1.00 equates to 100%, 0.10 equates to 10%, 0.01 equates to 1%, and 0.001 equates to 0.1%, then 0.002 is the equivalent of 0.2%. This matches with Table 15.3, which shows that the probability of the sample coming from the population in the null hypothesis is less than 1% but more than 0.1%. A probability of 0.2% lies within this range.
4. *DF = 9* This refers to the sampling distribution used in the hypothesis testing. Recall that 'DF' is shorthand for Degrees of Freedom. It describes the 'freedom' you have to put values into a column when the total is given. For example, as Figure 15.2 shows, there are 10 students whose total difference in marks is 60. You have the 'freedom' to put values into nine of the boxes, but the value in the 10th box is then fixed by the pre-set total (60). Thus, there are 9 degrees of freedom. When researchers calculated t tests manually, they had to identify the degrees of freedom in order to look up the correct row of the table of critical values. Note 1 to Table 15.5 shows that with a paired t test, the degrees of freedom are equal to the number of pairs of data minus 1. Thus, with 10 pairs of data, there are 9 degrees of freedom, and this is the row on the table that shows the relevant critical values.

| Free | + | Free | + | Free | + | Free | + | Free | + | Free | + | Free | + | Free | + | Free | + | Fixed | = 60 |

e.g.

| +3 | + | +9 | + | +5 | + | +7 | + | +11 | + | −2 | + | +2 | + | +6 | + | +7 | + | +12 | = 60 |

Figure 15.2   Degrees of freedom in Student's paired t test

The single variable used in the above example is the difference in assignment marks. This variable is based on the difference in each student's pair of assignment marks – one mark recorded before the typing course and one after. A test that uses information like this is a *paired t test* or *repeated measures t test* because, as is the case here, it often involves repeating the measurement of each individual in the sample. In the typing example, the two assignment marks for each student are paired when you calculate the difference between them.

Table 15.5   Critical values of Student's t

Degrees of freedom[1,2,3]	Probability level			
	5%	2%	1%	0.1%
9	2.26	2.82	3.25	4.78
10	2.23	2.76	3.17	4.59
12	2.18	2.68	3.06	4.32
14	2.15	2.62	2.98	4.14
16	2.12	2.58	2.92	4.02
18	2.10	2.55	2.88	3.92
20	2.09	2.53	2.85	3.85
30	2.04	2.46	2.75	3.65
60	2.00	2.39	2.66	3.46
120	1.98	2.36	2.62	3.37
Over 120	1.96	2.33	2.58	3.29

[1]Paired test DF = Number of pairs of data −1.
[2]One-sample test DF = Number of values −1.
[3]Unpaired test DF = (Number of values in group 1) − (Number of values in group 2).

Student's one-sample t test

A similar testing procedure is a *one-sample* Student's t test. Here you deal directly with just one original set of figures, or one sample. For example, a lecturer wants to test a manufacturer's claim that a particular type of projector bulb has an average life of 2000 hours. The lecturer tests 30 bulbs, and records how many hours each lasts. There is thus one set of figures, or one sample: the number of hours each of the 30 bulbs lasts. From these figures, the lecturer calculates that the mean bulb life is 1875 hours, with a standard deviation of 350 hours. How does the manufacturer's claim of an average bulb life of 2000 hours compare to this sample result?

BEHIND THE STATS

There is no simple answer to the question: 'Who invented the light bulb?' The first patent went to Englishman Frederick de Moleyns in 1841. But it became a practical proposition only in the 1870s when Sir Joseph Swan in England and Thomas Edison in the USA independently came up with the idea of using a vacuum inside the bulbs. Edison and Swan eventually combined to form what became General Electric. The first English football match played under lights was in 1878 in Sheffield. But a fire caused by lights led to a ban on floodlit football matches in the UK that was not lifted until 1956. In 1889, English county cricket team Surrey beat Yorkshire in the first ever cricket match played under lights. In 1892, the first floodlit American football match was 'abandoned because of a pylon placed dangerously in the middle of the pitch' (Henderson 2008).

The null hypothesis is based on the assumption that the manufacturer's claim is true. In other words, the null hypothesis is that the sample comes from a population of bulbs with a mean life of 2000 hours. The alternative hypothesis is based on the idea that the manufacturer's claim is not true: that the sample is not drawn from a population of bulbs with a mean life of 2000 hours (it might be less, or it might be more).

The procedure for a one-sample Student's t test is the same as that for a paired t test. It uses the three basic bits of information that you have about the sample:

1 Sample size (30)
2 Sample mean (1875)
3 Sample standard deviation (350).

First, you estimate the standard deviation of the population from the standard deviation of the sample (350) and size of the sample (30):

$$\text{SD of population} = \text{SD of sample} \times \sqrt{\frac{\text{Size of sample}}{\text{Size of sample} - 1}}$$

$$= 350 \times \sqrt{\frac{30}{29}} = 356$$

You then estimate the standard error of the sampling distribution from the standard deviation of the population (356) and the size of the sample (30):

$$\text{Standard error of sampling distribution} = \frac{\text{Standard deviation of population}}{\sqrt{\text{Size of sample}}}$$

$$= \frac{356}{\sqrt{30}} = 65$$

Finally, you find the position of the one sample taken in the sampling distribution that applies if the null hypothesis is correct. Recall that the null hypothesis says that the expected population mean is 2000 (the claim of the manufacturer). If the null hypothesis is correct, the sampling distribution of sample means should be centred on 2000. But the one sample taken has a mean of 1875. Thus, the observed sample mean is 125 less than the expected population mean (i.e. 2000 − 1875). You need to standardise this difference into a Student's t-score. This is simply how many standard errors the sample is away from the centre of the sampling distribution. The above equation shows that the standard error is 65. Thus, every 'standard deviation unit' is worth 65. A difference of 125 is thus 1.92 standard errors away from the centre of the sampling distribution (125 ÷ 65 = 1.92). In other words, the Student's t-score (disregarding the sign) is 1.92:

$$\text{Student's } t\text{-score} = \frac{\text{Observed sample mean} - \text{Expected population mean}}{\text{Standard error of sampling distribution of means}}$$

$$= \frac{1875 - 2000}{65} = \frac{-125}{65} = -1.92$$

Figure 15.3 shows the sampling distribution for a one-sample Student's *t* test with a sample size of 30, along with the critical value (2.05) at the 5% probability level. Table 15.6 also shows this 2.05 critical value, alongside critical values for the 2%, 1%, and 0.1% probability levels.

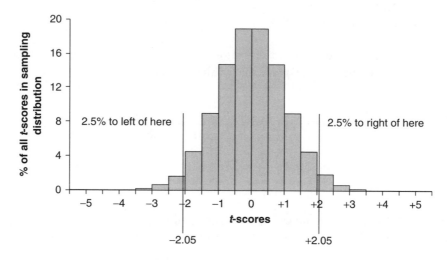

Figure 15.3 Sampling distribution of a Student's one-sample *t* test: one variable with 30 values

Table 15.6 Critical values of Student's one-sample *t* test: one variable with 30 values

Probability level	5%	2%	1%	0.1%
Critical value	2.05	2.46	2.76	3.66

↑

Calculated value of *t* = 1.92

Thus, the graph and table show that you need a calculated *t*-score (disregarding the sign) of at least 2.05 before you can reject the null hypothesis at the 5% significance level. In this example, the calculated value of *t* (disregarding the sign) is 1.92, which is *less* than the critical value. Thus, you retain the null hypothesis. The evidence from the sample is not strong enough to reject the manufacturer's claim of an average bulb life of 2000 hours. Table 15.7 summarises the bulb-testing research.

Table 15.7   Hypothesis testing using Student's one-sample *t*

Step		Bulb life result
1	Devise null hypothesis	Sample comes from the population specified by the manufacturer. The mean bulb life is 2000 hours
2	Devise alternative hypothesis	Sample does not come from the population specified by the manufacturer. The mean bulb life is not 2000 hours
3	Set significance level	5%
4	Calculate test statistic	One numerical variable (Life span of bulbs) with a sample size of 30: one-sample Student's *t* test = -1.92
5	Find probability level	Probability value is more than 5%
6	Make decision about null hypothesis	Significance level is 5% Probability value is more than 5% Retain null hypothesis
7	Make prediction about population	Sample comes from the population specified in the null hypothesis that there is a mean bulb life of 2000 hours

Hypotheses about two numerical variables – Pearson's *r*

This section looks again at Pearson's correlation coefficient, which is usually shortened to *Pearson's r*. This statistic first appeared in Chapter 9 as a measure of the correlation or association between two numerical variables. When knowledge of the values of the independent variable gives you absolutely no help in predicting values of the dependent variable, there is a *zero* association, and Pearson's *r* is 0. When knowledge of the values of the independent variable allows you to predict with perfect accuracy the values of the dependent variable, there is a *perfect correlation*, and Pearson's *r* is 1. If the dependent values decrease as the independent values increase, the direction of the association is *negative* and Pearson's *r* lies between −1 and 0. If the dependent values increase as the independent values increase, the direction of the correlation is *positive* and Pearson's *r* lies between 0 and +1.

You can also use Pearson's *r* in hypothesis testing to say something about the statistical association between the two variables in the population, based on the measured association in the sample. The example used in this section is about the association between exam preparation time and exam result. A random sample of 30 students from a population of 750 students complete a diary of how long they spend each day preparing for a particular exam. You add up each student's entries to find his or her total preparation time. You then use Pearson's correlation coefficient to measure the association between preparation time and exam result. The calculated *r* value is +0.50. How likely is it that an association also occurs in the student population as a whole?

Once again, the null hypothesis is that the sample comes from a population in which there is zero association between the two variables: (i) Preparation time (the independent variable) and (ii) Exam result (the dependent variable). When there is zero association, Pearson's *r* is 0. Thus, the null hypothesis is that the sample comes from a population in which r is 0. The alternative hypothesis, the logical opposite to the null hypothesis, is that the sample comes from a population in which there is an association between the two variables. Thus, the alternative hypothesis is that the sample comes from a population in which r is not 0.

What is the probability of drawing a sample of 30 with a Pearson's r value of 0.50 from a population with a Pearson's r value of 0? This sample is one of millions of possible samples of 30 students that you can draw from the population of 750 students. If you take all possible samples of 30, calculated the r value for each sample, and then plot all these r values, you end up with a sampling distribution centred on the population value of r. If the null hypothesis is correct, and there is zero association between the two variables in the population, the sampling distribution is centred on 0.

Statisticians have calculated the critical values of r for all sample sizes. Table 15.8 shows that when the sample size is 30, 5% of the r-scores in the sampling distribution are 0.36 or more (disregarding the sign); 2% are 0.42 or more; 1% are 0.46 or more; and 0.1% are 0.57 or more. Thus, a sample r-score of +0.50 is larger than the critical value at the 1% level (0.46) but smaller than the critical value at the 0.1% level (0.57). Thus, you reject the null hypothesis at the 1% significance level and support the alternative hypothesis: there *is* an association between the two variables, Preparation time and Exam result.

Table 15.8   Critical values of Pearson's r

Sample size	Probability level			
	5%	2%	1%	0.1%
10	0.63	0.72	0.77	0.87
20	0.44	0.52	0.56	0.68
30	0.36	0.42	0.46	0.57
40	0.31	0.37	0.40	0.50
50	0.28	0.33	0.36	0.45
60	0.25	0.30	0.33	0.41
70	0.24	0.28	0.31	0.39
80	0.22	0.26	0.29	0.36
90	0.21	0.25	0.27	0.34
100	0.20	0.23	0.26	0.32

You may recall from Chapter 9 that when you square Pearson's r you get a coefficient of determination. The sample has a Pearson's r-score of +0.50. This is equivalent to a coefficient of determination value of 0.25 (0.5×0.5). Because the coefficient of determination is a proportional reduction in error measure, a result of 0.25 means that knowledge of Preparation time values leads to a 25% in error when predicting Exam results. (Go back to Chapter 9 if you need to review this.) This means that there is a moderately strong association between the two variables in the sample. In terms of the direction of the association, the sample shows a positive association (r = +0.50). Consequently, you can expect a moderately strong positive association to occur in the population. Table 15.9 summarises the hypothesis-testing procedure using Pearson's r.

Table 15.9   Hypothesis testing using Pearson's r

Step		Exam preparation and exam result
1	Devise null hypothesis	Sample comes from the population in which there is no association between the two variables: (i) Exam preparation time and (ii) Exam result. In other words, Pearson's r is 0
2	Devise alternative hypothesis	Sample comes from a population in which there is an association between the two variables: (i) Exam preparation time and (ii) Exam result. In other words, Pearson's r is not 0
3	Set significance level	5%
4	Calculate test statistic	Two numerical variables with 30 values in each: Pearson's r is +0.60
5	Find probability level	Probability value is less than 1%
6	Make decision about null hypothesis	Significance level is 5% Probability value is less than 1% Reject null hypothesis
7	Make prediction about population	Sample comes from a population in which there is a moderately strong positive association between the two variables: as exam preparation time increases, so too does the exam result

Pearson's r and Student's t are both *parametric* tests. This means that, in theory, before using either as a test of significance, you should check to see that the population of each variable has a normal distribution — not an easy task when what you're doing is testing a hypothesis about the population! What often happens in practice is that researchers use the distribution of the values in their sample to estimate the distribution in the population. However, statisticians have found that Pearson's r and Student's t are *robust* statistics, meaning that researchers can use them even when the population is not normally distributed. It's only when the distribution of sample values is very skewed that researchers look around for alternative (i.e. *non-parametric*) tests of significance.

The previous chapter focused on testing hypotheses about categorical variables. This chapter focuses on numerical variables. The next (and final) chapter looks at those situations where one variable is categorical and the other variable is numerical. Again, the basic ideas remain the same. All that changes are the details of the calculations of the statistical tests.

SIXTEEN

Hypotheses about categories and numbers

```
| Chapter Overview |
```

This chapter will:

* Show how to test a hypothesis about one numerical variable and a categorical variable with only two categories using a *Student's unpaired t test*.
* Show how to test a hypothesis about one numerical variable and a categorical variable with two or more categories using *one-way analysis of variance*.

Chapter 14 focused on categorical variables, and Chapter 15 focused on numerical variables. This last chapter looks at how to test hypotheses about one numerical and one categorical variable. As Table 16.1 shows, it outlines two tests of significance: (i) Student's unpaired t test; and (ii) one-way analysis of variance.

Table 16.1   Some statistics for hypothesis testing

Variables	Statistical test
1 categorical	z test of sample %
	Chi-square goodness-of-fit test
2 categorical	Chi-square test for independence
1 numerical	Student's one-sample t test
	Student's paired t test
2 numerical	Pearson's correlation coefficient
1 categorical + 1 numerical two	**Student's unpaired t test (if categorical variable has just categories)**
	One-way analysis of variance (for any number of categories in categorical variable)

When there are just two groups in the categorical variable, the test often used is yet another version of Student's t, called the *unpaired t* test. It is also known as the *independent t* or *two-sample t* test. In contrast, analysis of variance can handle a categorical variable with any number of groups. One-way analysis of variance is also known as the *F ratio*, in honour of its originator, Ronald Fisher. Both F and t

lead to the same decision about the null hypothesis, and so it is not strictly necessary to know about the unpaired t test. However, as you'll see the unpaired t test in the literature, it's a good idea to be familiar with it.

BEHIND THE STATS

A contemporary of both Gosset and Pearson, Ronald Fisher was a British statistician whose abilities revealed themselves very early, as the following story shows. At the tender age of 3, he asked his nurse what was half of a half; he then asked what was half of a quarter; after a longer pause, he asked what was half of an eighth; and finally, after a long silence, he declared: 'Then, I suppose that a half of a sixteenth must be a thirty-toof' (Box, cited in Tankard, 1984: 113) Fisher had a long and illustrious career as a statistician. However, he wasn't always correct. He was sceptical of the survey evidence that tobacco smoking caused cancer, a topic that interested him because of 'his dislike and mistrust of puritanical tendencies of all kinds; and perhaps also the personal solace he had always found in tobacco' (Yates and Mather 1963: 106).

Student's unpaired t test

Imagine that a lecturer teaching Social Statistics 101 has the choice of two statistical software packages, Superstat and Goldstat. She randomly divides her students into

Table 16.2   Students: exam mark, by software

Student ID	Software used	Exam mark	Mean mark	Standard deviation
A	Superstat	60		
B	Superstat	65		
C	Superstat	65		
D	Superstat	70		
E	Superstat	70	70	5.77
F	Superstat	70		
G	Superstat	75		
H	Superstat	75		
I	Superstat	80		
J	Goldstat	55		
K	Goldstat	59		
L	Goldstat	59		
M	Goldstat	63		
N	Goldstat	63	63	4.62
O	Goldstat	63		
P	Goldstat	67		
Q	Goldstat	67		
R	Goldstat	71		

Source: Hypothetical

two groups. Each group covers the same course material in exactly the same way except that one group uses Superstat and the other uses Goldstat. At the end of the course, students in both groups attempt the same exam. Table 16.2 shows the software used by each student and his or her exam mark.

Table 16.2 shows two things about each of the 18 students: (i) the software he or she used (Superstat, Goldstat); and (ii) his or her exam mark (e.g. 60, 55). Thus, there are two variables. The independent variable is Software. It is a categorical variable with two categories. The dependent variable is Exam mark. It is measured by numbers, and so is a numerical variable. A Student's unpaired t test is an appropriate test of significance.

You can tell just by looking down the two columns that, overall, students using Superstat did better than those using Goldstat. However, is the difference between the two groups sufficiently large for you to be confident that Superstat really is the better package? The unpaired t test will help you decide.

The prediction you test is that among all students there is no difference in the results of those using Superstat and those using Goldstat. The null hypothesis is that the two groups of results are samples from identical populations. If the populations are identical, their means are the same. Thus, the null hypothesis is that the population mean of the Superstat group of students is the same as the population mean of the Goldstat group of students. The alternative hypothesis, the logical opposite of the null hypothesis, is that the two means are different.

The unpaired Student's t test is based on the same rationale as the paired and one-sample t tests: you compare the observed sample result to the expected population result, and standardise the difference between the two in terms of the standard error of the sampling distribution:

$$\text{Unpaired } t = \frac{\begin{array}{c}\text{Observed difference} \\ \text{in sample means}\end{array} - \begin{array}{c}\text{Expected difference in} \\ \text{in population means}\end{array}}{\begin{array}{c}\text{Standard error of sampling} \\ \text{distribution of differences in means}\end{array}}$$

You calculate the *observed difference in sample means* from the exam marks of the two groups. As Table 16.2 shows, the Superstat group mean is 70.0, and the Goldstat group mean is 63.0. Thus the observed difference between the sample means is 7.0.

You decide on the *expected difference in population means* from what you expect if the null hypothesis is correct, and that the two groups are drawn from identical populations. If they are identical, then their means are the same, and thus the expected difference between the means is 0.

Calculate the *standard error* of the sampling distribution of each of the group means in the usual way:

1 Estimate the standard deviation of the population from the standard deviation of the sample:

$$\text{SD of population} = \text{SD of sample} \times \sqrt{\frac{\text{Size of sample}}{\text{Size of sample} - 1}}$$

2 Estimate the standard error of the sampling distribution of the means from the standard deviation of the population and the size of the sample:

$$\text{Standard error of sampling distribution of mean} = \frac{\text{Standard deviation of population}}{\sqrt{\text{Size of sample}}}$$

Table 16.3 shows the calculations of the standard errors of the group means, and then how to combine them to find the standard error of the differences in group means.

You now have the three statistics needed to work out the unpaired t score:

1 Observed difference in sample means (7.0)
2 Expected difference in population means (0)
3 Standard error of sampling distribution of difference in sample means (2.61):

$$\text{Student's } t = \frac{\begin{array}{c}\text{Observed difference} \\ \text{in sample means}\end{array} - \begin{array}{c}\text{Expected difference} \\ \text{in population means}\end{array}}{\begin{array}{c}\text{Standard error of sampling distribution} \\ \text{of difference in sample means}\end{array}}$$

$$= \frac{7 - 0}{2.61} = 2.68$$

Table 16.3   Standard errors for unpaired t test

Superstat group	Goldstat group
1 Standard deviation of population	1 Standard deviation of population
$= \text{SD sample} \times \sqrt{\dfrac{\text{Size of sample}}{\text{Size of sample} - 1}}$	$= \text{SD sample} \times \sqrt{\dfrac{\text{Size of sample}}{\text{Size of sample} - 1}}$
$= 5.77 \times \sqrt{\dfrac{9}{8}} = 6.12$	$= 4.62 \times \sqrt{\dfrac{9}{8}} = 4.90$
2 SE of Superstat group	2 SE of Goldstat group
$= \dfrac{\text{SD of population}}{\sqrt{\text{Size of sample}}}$	$= \dfrac{\text{SD of population}}{\sqrt{\text{Size of sample}}}$
$= \dfrac{6.12}{\sqrt{9}} = 2.04$	$= \dfrac{4.90}{\sqrt{9}} = 1.63$

$$\text{SE of difference in group means} = \sqrt{(\text{SE of group 1})^2 + (\text{SE of group 2})^2}$$

$$= \sqrt{(\text{SE Superstat})^2 + (\text{SE Goldstat})^2}$$

$$= \sqrt{2.04^2 + 1.63^2} = 2.61$$

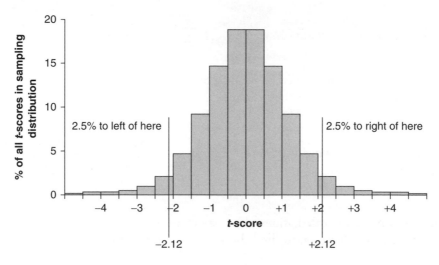

Figure 16.1   Sampling distribution of unpaired Student's *t*: two groups, nine individuals in each

As always, the next step is to locate the position of the calculated *t*-score (2.68) on the relevant sampling distribution. You do this to find the probability of such a sample result occurring if the two groups come from two identical populations, as specified in the null hypothesis. Figure 16.1 shows the relevant sampling distribution. For clarity, it shows only one critical value: 5% of all results (2.5% in each tail) have an absolute *t*-score of at least 2.12. Table 16.4 shows this and other critical values of *t* when there are nine individuals in each of the two groups.

The calculated *t*-score (2.68) is larger than the critical value at the 2% probability level (2.58) but smaller than the critical value at the 1% level (2.92). Thus, there is less than a 2% chance that these two samples come from identical populations, as specified in the null hypothesis. Using a 5% significance level, you reject the null hypothesis and support the alternative hypothesis: the Superstat population mean is not the same as the Goldstat population mean. The sample result shows that the Superstat group did *better* than the Goldstat group, and this is what you expect to find among students as a whole.

The sampling distribution and associated critical values shown in Figure 16.1 and Table 16.4 apply when the unpaired Student's *t* calculation is based on two groups each with nine values. Groups of different sizes have different sampling distributions. Fortunately, statisticians have worked out the exact shape of the

Table 16.4   Critical values of unpaired Student's *t*: two groups, nine individuals in each

Probability level	5%	2%	1%	0.1%
Critical value of *t*	2.12	2.58	2.92	4.02

↑

Calculated value of *t* = 2.68

sampling distribution for every possible combination of group sizes. Consequently, software packages such as SPSS and Minitab give you not only the Student's t result, but also the probability of drawing the sample from the population in the null hypothesis. For example, your printout of results from the software package might be as follows:

T test of difference = 0: T-Value – 2.68, P-Value = 0.017, DF = 16

1 *T test of difference = 0* This refers to the null hypothesis that there is zero (0) difference between the two population means.
2 *T-Value = 2.68* This is the calculated t test statistic of 2.68.
3 *P-Value = 0.017* This is the probability value. It's shown as a proportion (0.017) being the equivalent of 1.7%. This matches with Table 16.3, which tells us that the probability of the sample coming from the population in the null hypothesis is less than 2% but more than 1%.
4 *DF = 16* This refers to the sampling distribution used in the hypothesis testing. Recall that 'DF' is shorthand for Degrees of Freedom. It describes the 'freedom' you have to put values into a column when the total is given. For example, as Figure 16.2(a) shows, in the Superstat software group there are nine students whose total exam result is 630. You have the 'freedom' to put values into eight of the boxes, but the value in the ninth box is then fixed by the pre-set total. Thus, there are 8 degrees of freedom for the Superstat group. In addition, there are nine students and thus 8 degrees of freedom for the Goldstat group (Figure 16.2b). Overall, therefore, there are 16 (8 + 8) degrees of freedom. When researchers calculated t tests manually, they had to identify the degrees of freedom in order to look up the correct row of the table of critical values (see Table 15.5).

The above example tests the null hypothesis that there is no *difference* between the population means of the groups (e.g. Superstat users and Goldstat users).

(a) Superstat group

| Free | + | Free | + | Free | + | Free | + | Free | + | Free | + | Free | + | Free | + | Fixed | = 630 |

e.g.

| 60 | + | 65 | + | 65 | + | 70 | + | 70 | + | 70 | + | 75 | + | 75 | + | (80) | = 630 |

(b) Goldstat group

| Free | + | Free | + | Free | + | Free | + | Free | + | Free | + | Free | + | Free | + | Fixed | = 567 |

e.g.

| 55 | + | 59 | + | 59 | + | 63 | + | 63 | + | 63 | + | 67 | + | 67 | + | (71) | = 567 |

Figure 16.2   Degrees of freedom in unpaired t test

Table 16.5   Different ways of organising data: Exam mark and Software

Null hypothesis A No difference between groups		Null hypothesis B No association between variables	
Superstat	Goldstat	Software	Mark
60	55	Superstat	60
65	59	Superstat	65
65	59	Superstat	65
70	63	Superstat	70
70	63	Superstat	70
70	63	Superstat	70
75	67	Superstat	75
75	67	Superstat	75
80	71	Superstat	80
		Goldstat	55
		Goldstat	59
		Goldstat	59
		Goldstat	63
		Goldstat	63
		Goldstat	63
		Goldstat	67
		Goldstat	67
		Goldstat	71

Although the no-difference hypothesis is easier to understand, you can equally well start with the null hypothesis that the sample comes from a population in which there is no *association* between the two variables, Exam mark and Software. In other words, the null hypothesis is that knowledge of each student's software group gives you no extra help in predicting his or her exam mark. This involves simply a change of perspective, as Table 16.5 shows.

Thus, you know from the unpaired *t* test that the sample results show that it is likely there is an association between the two variables in the population. However, you do not have any direct measure of the strength of this association. Remember that the *t* test shows only the probability of the sample coming from a population in which there is *zero* association between the variables. What you need is a direct measure of the strength of the association.

Chapter 9 showed that the eta-squared correlation coefficient measures the association between one numerical and one categorical variable. When the categorical variable has only two groups, eta squared is often referred to as the *point biserial correlation coefficient*. You calculate it as follows:

$$\text{Eta-squared (or point biserial) correlation coefficient} = \frac{t^2}{t^2 + df}$$

In the software example, t is 2.68, and there are 16 degrees of freedom. The eta-squared calculation is therefore:

$$\text{Eta-squared correlation coefficient} = \frac{t^2}{t^2 + df} = \frac{2.68^2}{2.68^2 + 16} = \frac{7.18}{23.18} = 0.31$$

Eta squared is a proportional reduction in error measure. Thus 0.31 shows that there is a 31% reduction in error when you predict exam marks using knowledge about the software. In other words, there is a moderately strong association between these two variables. The unpaired t test shows that an association of similar strength is likely to occur among all students, not just those in the sample. Table 16.6 summarises the statistical software research using Student's unpaired t test.

One-way analysis of variance

An unpaired Student's t test is suitable for the data in the section above because the categorical variable has only two categories. However, when there are more than two categories, you need to use one-way analysis of variance. I'll

Table 16.6   Hypothesis testing using unpaired t test

Step	Statistical software: Superstat v Goldstat
1 Devise null hypothesis	Samples come from identical populations, and so there is no difference in the two group means (i.e. the difference in exam scores of the Superstat and Goldstat groups is 0)
2 Devise alternative hypothesis	Samples come from populations in which there is a difference in the two group means (i.e. the difference in exam scores of the Superstat and Goldstat groups is not 0)
3 Set significance level	5%
4 Calculate test statistic	One categorical variable (Software) with two categories and one numerical variable (Exam mark) with a total sample size of 18: unpaired t test = 2.61
5 Find probability level	Probability value is less than 2%
6 Make decision about null hypothesis	Significance level is 5%
	Probability value is less than 2%
	Reject null hypothesis and accept alternative hypothesis
7 Make prediction about populations	Samples come from populations in which there is a difference in the exam scores of the Superstat and Goldstat students. Sample results show that students using Superstat (mean = 70.0) did better than students using Goldstat (mean = 63.0). This is also likely to occur in the population. Eta-squared correlation coefficient (0.31) shows a moderately strong association between the two variables

continue with the same sort of example as before, but with software from three companies.

A lecturer wants to evaluate three statistical software packages (A, B, C) to see which is best for his students. He randomly places 5 students in group A, 5 in group B, and 5 in group C. Each group covers the same material in the same way apart from the statistical software used. At the end of the course, an exam might produce the results shown in Table 16.7.

The difference in marks *between* the groups stands out because there is no difference in the marks *within* each group (e.g. all group A students scored 55). Or, expressed slightly differently, there is between-group variation but no within-group variation. Software C is the best: all students in group C have a mark of 75, compared to 65 for all students in group B, and 55 for all in group A.

Of course, you don't expect all students in the same group to have exactly the same mark. Students differ in terms of their ability and motivation, and these differences will be reflected in differences in their marks. Table 16.8 shows a more realistic set of results, with variations in marks both between groups and within groups. Although the means of the three groups are the same as before (55, 65, 75), the variation in marks within each group results in a lot of overlap in marks between groups. For example, each group includes a student with a mark of 65.

Table 16.7   Between-group variation

Software group		
A	**B**	**C**
55	65	75
55	65	75
55	65	75
55	65	75
55	65	75

Table 16.8 Between-group variation and within-group variation

| Software used | | |
A	B	C
45	55	65
50	60	70
55	65	75
60	70	80
65	75	85

Thus, there are two types of variation in the exam marks:

1 *Between-group variation* appears very clearly in Table 16.7 and rather less clearly in Table 16.8.
2 *Within-group variation* is absent from Table 16.7, but appears in Table 16.8.

The lecturer is interested in the between-group variation – he wants to find out about the difference in the marks of the three groups so that he can make a decision about what software to use. The prediction he tests is that among all students there is no difference in the results, regardless of whether students use software package A, B, or C. The null hypothesis is based on the idea that the three groups of results are samples from identical populations. If the populations are identical, then their means are the same. The null hypothesis is that the mean of population A is equal to the mean of population B and the mean of population C.

If you reject the null hypothesis that the groups are all from identical populations, you support the alternative hypothesis that the groups are not all from identical populations. Note that the alternative hypothesis is not that the groups are *all* from different populations. The exact wording is important. Consider the following figures:

A	B	C
52	52	56
54	54	61
56	56	67
60	60	70
64	64	74
67	67	81
67	67	81

Using one-way analysis of variance, you reject the null hypothesis that the three groups come from identical populations. However, this is not to say that the three groups *all* come from different populations – indeed, groups A and B look remarkably similar!

Of course, even if the three samples *have* been drawn from identical populations, you are likely to get some differences between groups, just as you are likely to get differences within each group. But if all the samples have been drawn from identical populations, the average variation in scores *between* the groups should be similar to the average variation in scores *within* the groups. In contrast, if the type of software really does make a difference then you would expect the between-group variation to be larger than the within-group variation.

Analysis of variance simply compares these two types of variation. The test statistic is often referred to as an *F ratio* because it measures the ratio between the two types of variation:

$$F \text{ ratio} = \frac{\text{Between-group variation}}{\text{Within-group variation}}$$

Under the null hypothesis, the *F* ratio should be close to 1 because the between-group variation should be about equal to the within-group variation. An *F* ratio of 2 means that the between-group variation is twice that of the within-group variation. Similarly, an *F* ratio of 4 means that the between-group variation is four times that of the within-group variation. Thus, the larger the *F* ratio, the greater the chance that the groups have not all been drawn from identical populations, and therefore the greater the probability that you will reject the null hypothesis. To calculate an *F* ratio, you need measures of the between-group variation and within-group variation. In analysis of variance, variation (not surprisingly) is measured by the *variance*.

The first step in calculating the *within-group variation* is to find the sum of squares. Recall that the sum of squares is the total (or sum) of deviations of the individual values from the mean, each of these deviations being squared to get rid of any minus signs. Table 16.9 shows the results of all the within-group sum of squares calculations.

Table 16.9   Within-group variance

Group A		Group B		Group C	
Score	(Score – Group mean)^2	Score	(Score – Group mean)^2	Score	(Score – Group mean)^2
45	$(45 - 55)^2 = 100$	55	$(55 - 65)^2 = 100$	65	$(65 - 75)^2 = 100$
50	$(50 - 55)^2 = 25$	60	$(60 - 65)^2 = 25$	70	$(70 - 75)^2 = 25$
55	$(55 - 55)^2 = 0$	65	$(65 - 65)^2 = 0$	75	$(75 - 75)^2 = 0$
60	$(60 - 55)^2 = 25$	70	$(70 - 65)^2 = 25$	80	$(80 - 75)^2 = 25$
65	$(65 - 55)^2 = 100$	75	$(75 - 65)^2 = 100$	85	$(85 - 75)^2 = 100$
	Sum of squares = 250		Sum of squares = 250		Sum of squares = 250

Within-group sum of squares = 250 + 250 + 250 = 750

$$\text{Within-group variance} = \frac{\text{Within-group sum of squares}}{\text{Sum of (Number of individuals in each group} - 1)} = \frac{750}{4 + 4 + 4} = \frac{750}{12} = 62.5$$

You then find the mean of all the sum of squares values. Usually, to find a mean you simply divide the total by the number of values. However, although this procedure accurately measures the variance of the *sample*, it tends to underestimate the variance of the *population* – and the population is what you're interested in. To counteract this tendency, you reduce each group size by 1 before calculating the variance. The final row of Table 16.9 shows that the within-group variation is 62.5.

Table 16.10 shows a similar procedure to calculate the *between-group variation*. The mean used here is the overall mean (65) – in other words, the sum of all the exam marks (975) divided by the total number of students (15). The individual values are the *group* means (A – 55, B – 65, C = 75). Thus, the overall mean is subtracted from each group mean, and the result is squared to get rid of any minus signs. Recall that the within-group sum of squares values are based on the number of exam scores in each group. To allow a meaningful comparison, the between-group sum of squares values have to be based on the same number of deviation values. Table 16.10 shows the between-group sum of squares calculations.

Dividing the between-group sum of squares total by the number of groups gives the sample variance. However, because as before the sample variance underestimates the population variance, you divide the sum of squares by *one less* than the number of groups in the sample. In this example, the between-group sum of squares total is 1000, and there are three groups (A, B, C). Table 16.10 shows that the estimate of the between-group variance in the population is 500.

As the between-group variance is 500 and the within-group variance is 62.5, the *F* ratio is:

$$F \text{ ratio} = \frac{\text{Between-group variance}}{\text{Within-group variance}} = \frac{500}{62.5} = 8.00$$

An *F* ratio of 2 means that the between-group variation is twice the within-group variation. Similarly, an *F* ratio of 4 means that the between-group variation is four times the within-group variation. Thus, the larger the *F* ratio, the greater the chance that the groups have not all been drawn from identical populations, and therefore the greater the probability that the null hypothesis will be rejected.

Table 16.10   Between-group variance

Group	Group mean (GM)	Overall mean (OM)	$(GM - OM)^2$	Group size	$(GM - OM)^2$ × Group size
A	55	65	$(55 - 65)^2 = 100$	5	$100 \times 5 = 500$
B	65	65	$(65 - 65)^2 = 0$	5	$0 \times 5 = 0$
C	75	65	$(75 - 65)^2 = 100$	5	$100 \times 5 = 500$
					Between-group sum of squares = 1000

$$\text{Between-group variance} = \frac{\text{Sum of squares}}{\text{Number of groups} - 1} = \frac{1000}{3 - 1} = \frac{1000}{2} = 500$$

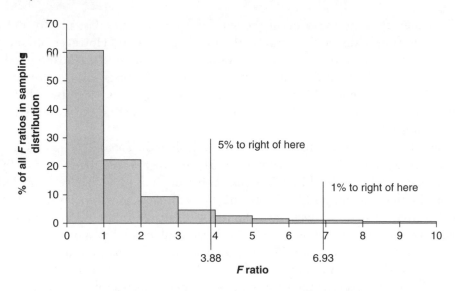

Figure 16.3   Sampling distribution of Fisher's F ratio: three groups, five individuals in each group

An F ratio of 8.00 shows that the between-group variation is eight times larger than the within-group variation. Thus, it seems very likely that you will reject the null hypothesis and support the alternative that the groups have not all come from identical populations.

Because of the way F is calculated, it is impossible to have a negative result: both the between-group and within-group variances are based on sums of squares, and thus cannot be negative. Thus, like chi-square, the sampling distribution of F starts at 0. Remember that the sampling distribution shows all possible sample results of F when the groups are drawn from identical populations. Thus, you would expect most of the F ratios to be very low, reflecting small sample differences between the groups.

Figure 16.3 and Table 16.11 show the sampling distribution of F when there are three groups and a total of 15 individuals. Like chi-square, the distribution shows a marked right-hand skew. Indeed, only 5% of F values are 3.88 or more, and only 1% are 6.93 or more. In other words, at the 5% probability level the critical value is 3.88, and at the 1% level the critical value is 6.93. The sample result (8.00) is larger than the critical value at the 1% probability level (6.93) but smaller than the critical value at the 0.1% probability level (12.97). Thus, there is less than a 1% chance that the null hypothesis is correct. With a 5% significance level you reject the null hypothesis and support the alternative hypothesis: the groups are not all from identical populations. In other words, there is some difference in the mean results of students using software A, software B, and software C.

The sampling distribution of the F ratio is appropriate for this statistical problem, but like Student's t and chi-square there is a range of sampling distributions of F. Fortunately, statisticians have worked out the exact shape of each.

Table 16.11   Critical values of Fisher's F ratio: three groups, five individuals in each

Probability level	5%	2%	1%	0.1%
Critical value of t	3.88	5.52	6.93	12.97

↑

Calculated value of F = 8.00

Consequently, software packages give you not only the F ratio, but also the probability of drawing the sample from the population in the null hypothesis. For example, your printout of results may include the following information:

F = 8.00, P = 0.006, DF = 2 (Factor), 12 (Error)

1 F = 8.00 This is the F ratio test statistic.
2 P = 0.006 This is the exact probability of drawing the sample from the population specified in the null hypothesis. If a probability value of 1.00 equals 100%, and 0.01 equals 1%, then 0.006 equals 0.6%. This matches the conclusion above that the probability of drawing the sample from the population in the null hypothesis is less than 1% but more than 0.1%.
3 DF = 2 (Factor), 12 (Error) These are the degrees of freedom (DF) values. With the F ratio there are two degrees of freedom values, one for the number of groups and the other for the number of individuals. The '2 (Factor)' or between-group DF value is one less than the number of groups (A, B, C). The '12 (Error)' or within-group DF value is the total number of individuals (15) less the number of groups (3). If you calculate the F ratio manually, the

Table 16.12   Critical values of F

Within-group DF[2]	Between-group degrees of freedom[1]									
	1		2		3		4		5	
10	4.96[3]	10.04[4]	4.10	7.56	3.71	6.55	3.48	5.99	3.33	5.64
12	4.75	9.33	3.88	6.93	3.49	5.95	3.26	5.41	3.11	5.06
14	4.60	8.86	3.74	6.51	3.34	5.56	3.11	5.03	2.96	4.69
16	4.49	8.53	3.63	6.23	3.24	5.29	3.01	4.77	2.85	4.44
18	4.41	8.28	3.55	6.01	3.16	5.09	2.93	4.58	2.77	4.25
20	4.35	8.10	3.49	5.85	3.10	4.94	2.87	4.43	2.71	4.10
40	4.08	7.31	3.23	5.18	2.84	4.31	2.61	3.83	2.45	3.51
60	4.00	7.08	3.15	4.98	2.76	4.13	2.52	3.65	2.37	3.34
80	3.96	6.69	3.11	4.88	2.72	4.04	2.48	3.56	2.33	3.25
100	3.94	6.90	3.09	4.82	2.70	3.98	2.46	3.51	2.30	3.20

[1] Between-group degrees of freedom: Number of groups − 1.
[2] Within-group degrees of freedom: Total number of individuals − Number of groups.
[3] Critical values at 5% probability level are in roman font.
[4] Critical values at 1% probability level are in italic font.

final step is to find the probability value using a table of critical values. You need the two degrees of freedom values to identify the correct critical values. Table 16.12 shows that when the within-group degrees of freedom value is 12 and the between-group degrees of freedom value is 2, the 5% critical value is 3.88 and the 1% critical value is 6.93.

Thus, the F test shows that there is some difference in the mean results of students using software A, software B, and software C. Of course, the lecturer wants to go further than this – he wants to find out the *best* software to use. The simplest solution is to look at the mean exam scores of the three groups: group A, 55%; group B, 65%; and group C, 75%. Clearly, group C students did best, and so the lecturer is likely to choose this software.

However, results are not always so clear cut. For example, what if the means had been as follows: A, 55%; B, 70%; and C, 75%? The F ratio might still lead to a rejection of the null hypothesis that the samples have been drawn from identical populations. But you can't be certain that there is a difference in the populations between software B (with a mean of 70%) and C (with a mean of 75%). You could go on to calculate an unpaired Student's t on these two groups. There are some technical problems with doing this, but overall it's a reasonable course of action, particularly if there are only three groups in the categorical variable.

If there's a difference between the groups (A, B, C) then there's a statistical association between the variables (Software, Marks). However, the F test is not an ideal measure of the strength of the association. This is because it shows the probability of the sample coming from a population in which there is *zero* association between the variables. What you need is a direct measure of the strength of the association.

You can use the eta-squared correlation coefficient again to measure the strength of the association between the variables. You calculate eta-squared directly from the F ratio (8.00) and the between-groups degrees of freedom (2) and the within-groups degrees of freedom (12):

$$\text{Eta-squared correlation coefficient} = \frac{\text{Between groups } df \times F}{\text{Between groups } (df \times F) + \text{Within group } df}$$

$$= \frac{28.00}{(2 \times 8.00) + 12} = \frac{16.00}{28.00} = 0.57$$

Eta squared is a proportional reduction in error measure, varying between 0 and 1. An eta-squared result of 0 indicates a zero association, and an eta-squared result of 1 indicates a perfect association. An eta-squared result of 0.57 means that there is a 57% reduction in error when you predict exam marks using knowledge about the software. In other words, there is quite a strong association between the two variables. However, notice that you can't say anything about the *direction* of the association because the Software variable is made up of unordered categories. Table 16.13 summarises the software research using analysis of variance.

Table 16.13   Hypothesis testing using one-way analysis of variance

Step	Statistical software: A v B v C
1 Devise null hypothesis	Samples come from identical populations. Thus, there is no difference in the means of the exam scores of software groups A, B, and C
2 Devise alternative hypothesis	Samples do not come from identical populations. Thus, there is a difference in the means of the exam scores of software groups A, B, and C
3 Set significance level	5%
4 Calculate test statistic	One categorical variable (Software) with three categories and one numerical variable (Exam marks) with a sample size of 15: F test = 8.00
5 Find probability level	Probability value is less than 1%
6 Make decision about null hypothesis	Significance level is 5% Probability value is less than 1% Reject null hypothesis and accept alternative hypothesis
7 Make prediction about population	Samples do not come from identical populations. Sample results show that the exam marks of Group C were highest (mean = 75%) and this is likely to occur in the population. Eta-squared correlation coefficient (0.57) shows quite a strong association between the two variables in the sample, and this is also likely in the population

If you have worked your way through this and the previous three chapters, you should now be very familiar with hypothesis testing. You have looked at a range of tests of significance: z tests, chi-square tests, Student's t tests, Pearson's r, and finally the one-way analysis of variance. These tests are just the tip of a statistical iceberg. For example, one best-selling book has the title *100 Statistical Tests* (Kanji 2006). All tests are different in detail, but all are based on the same general idea of using the one known sample result to say something about the unknown population by using a sampling distribution. However, the general ideas about hypothesis testing that you now know apply regardless of the specific significance test. You are thus in a good position to tackle hypothesis testing with confidence!

References

AASHTO (American Association of State Highway and Transport Officials) 2004, *A Policy on Geometric Design of Highways and Streets* (5th edn), AASHTO, Washington, DC.

ABS (Australian Bureau of Statistics) 2006, *Census, 8 August 2006, Household form*, viewed 22 June 2009, http://www.abs.gov.au/websitedbs/d3310114.nsf/4a256353001af3ed 4b2562bb00121564/d14318a2e9282072ca25715d00177d17/$FILE/HHF%202006%20 Sample%20only.pdf.

ABS (Australian Bureau of Statistics) 2007, *Household income and income distribution, Australia, 2005–06* (Cat. no. 6523.0), ABS, Canberra.

ADS (American Dialect Society) 2007, *'Plutoed' voted 2007 Word of the Year*, ADS, 1 July 2009, http://www.americandialect.org/Word-of-the-Year_2006.pdf.

Atkin, R 2008, *Fashion at Wimbledon*, All England Lawn Tennis Club, viewed 15 February 2008, http://www.wimbledon.org/en_GB/about/history/fashion.html.

Barry, JV 2006, 'Kelly, Edward (Ned) (1855–1880)', *Australian dictionary of biography*, online edition, viewed 1 July 2009, http://www.adb.online.anu.edu.au/biogs/A050009b.htm.

BBFC (British Board of Film Classification) 2009, *Statistics for film works processed in 2007*, BBFC, viewed 23 June 2009, http://www.bbfc.co.uk/statistics/index.php.

Blanchflower, DG and Oswald, AJ 2008, 'Is well-being U-shaped over the life cycle?', *Social Science & Medicine*, vol. 66, pp. 1733–49.

Box Office Mojo 2009, *Adjusting for ticket price inflation*, Box Office Mojo, viewed 25 June 2009, http://www.boxofficemojo.com/about/adjuster.htm.

Bridgstock, M 2003, 'Paranormal beliefs among science students', *Skeptic* [Australia], vol. 23, no. 1, pp. 6–10.

Bryson, B 1990, *Mother Tongue: The English Language*, Penguin, London.

Cannell, CF 1985, 'Interviewing in telephone surveys', in TW Beed and RJ Stimson (eds), *Survey Interviewing: Theory and techniques*, George Allen & Unwin, Sydney, pp. 63–84.

CCA (Cancer Council of Australia) 2009, *SunSmart*, CCA, viewed 24 June 2009, http://www.cancer.org.au/cancersmartlifestyle/SunSmart.htm.

CIA (Central Intelligence Agency) 2009, *World factbook: country comparison—area*, CIA, viewed 23 June 2009, https://www.cia.gov/library/publications/the-world-factbook/ rankorder/2147rank.html/.

CoE (Council of Europe) 2009, *Council of Europe in brief*, viewed 23 June 2009, http://www.coe.int/T/e/Com/about_coe/.

Crystal, D 2003, *The Cambridge Encyclopedia of the English Language* (2nd edn), Cambridge University Press, Cambridge.

CSBN (Committee on Small Body Nomenclature) 2007, *Names of minor planets*, University of Maryland, viewed 30 June 2009, http://www.ss.astro.umd.edu/IAU/csbn/mpnames.shtml.

Dewdney, AK 1993, *200% of Nothing*, Wiley, New York.

Dexter, G 2007, 'A classic by any other name', *Telegraph.co.uk*, 18 November, viewed 1 July 2009, http://www.telegraph.co.uk/arts/main.jhtml?xml=/arts/2007/11/ 18/sv_catch.xml.

Dutton, G 2006, 'Eyre, Edward John (1815–1901)' *Australian dictionary of biography online edition*, viewed 1 July 2009, http://www.adb.online.anu.edu.au/biogs/A010346b.htm? hilite=Eyre.

Egan, ME and Schoenberger, CR (eds) 2008, *The world's 100 most powerful women*, Forbes, viewed 26 June 2009, http://www.forbes.com/2008/08/27/most-powerful-women biz powerwomen08-cz_me_cs_0827women_land.html.

ESC (Eurovision Song Contest) 2009, viewed 23 June 2009, http://www.eurovision.tv/page/home.

EURF (European Union Road Federation) 2008, *European road statistics 2008*, EURF, Brussels, viewed 25 June 2009, http://www.irfnet.eu/en/2008-road-statistics/.

Eyre, EJ 1845, *Journals of Expeditions of Discovery... Vol. II*, T. and W. Boone, London (Australiana Facsimile Editions No. 7, Libraries Board of South Australia, 1964).

Freudenburg, WR and Davidson, DJ 2007, 'Nuclear families and nuclear risks: the effects of gender, geography, and progeny on attitudes toward a nuclear waste facility', *Rural Sociology*, vol. 72, no. 2, pp. 215–43.

Gallup 2007, *Attitudes on issues related to EU energy policy: analytical report*, European Commission, viewed 1 July 2009, http://ec.europa.eu/public_opinion/flash/fl206a_en.pdf.

Gould, SJ 1985, 'The median isn't the message', *Discover*, June, pp. 40–2.

Guinness nd, *The story*, Guinness & Co, viewed 29 June 2009, http://www2.guinness.com/en-IE/Pages/thestory-1900.aspx/.

Heller, J 1961, *Catch-22*, Simon & Schuster, New York.

Helliwell, JF 2006, 'Well-being, social integration and public policy: what's new?', *Economic Journal*, vol. 116, March, pp. C34–45.

Henderson, J 2008, 'End of the dark ages', *Observer*, 9 March, viewed 1 July 2009, http://sport.guardian.co.uk/motorsport/story/0,,2263676,00.html.

Hibbeln, JR, Nieminen, LRG, and Lands, WEM 2004, 'Increasing homicide rates and linoleic acid consumption among five western countries, 1961–2000', *Lipids*, vol. 39, no. 12, pp. 1207–13.

Highway Code 2009, Directgov, viewed 29 June 2009, http://www.direct.gov.uk/en/TravelAndTransport/Highwaycode/DG_070202.

Huff, D 1954, *How To Lie With Statistics*, Victor Gollancz, London.

IAU (International Astronomical Union) 2008, *News release – IAU0804: plutoed chosen as name for solar system objects like Pluto*, IAU, viewed 1 July 2009, http://www.iau.org/public_press/news/release/iau0804/.

IMDb (Internet Movie Database) 2009a, *All-time worldwide box office*, IMDb, viewed 22 June 2009, http://us.imdb.com/boxoffice/alltimegross?region=world-wide.

IMDb (Internet Movie Database) 2009b, *Country browser*, IMDb, viewed 23 June 2009, http://us.imdb.com/Sections/Countries/.

Ipsos MORI 2007, *Public attitudes to the nuclear industry*, Nuclear Industry Association, viewed 15 January 2008, http://www.ipsos-mori.com/polls/2007/niauk2.shtml.

Jones, F 2008, 'The effects of taxes and benefits on household income, 2006/07', *Economic & Labour Market Review*, vol. 2, no. 7, pp. 37–47, viewed 26 June 2009, http://www.statistics.gov.uk/cci/article.asp?id=2022.

Kanji, GK 2006, *100 Statistical Tests* (3rd edn), Sage, London.

Kincaid, P 1986, *The Rule of the Road: An international guide to history and practice*, Greenwood Press, New York.

Kish, L 1965, *Survey Sampling*, Wiley, New York.

Lucas, B 2005, *Which side of the road do they drive on?*, viewed 30 June 2009, http://brianlucas.ca/roadside/.

Lyons, L 2005, *Paranormal beliefs come (super)naturally to some*, Gallup, viewed 30 June 2009, http://www.gallup.com/poll/19558/Paranormal-Beliefs-Come-SuperNaturally-Some.aspx.

Malkin, B 2007, 'Guinness "may be good for you" after all', *Electronic Telegraph*, 12 September, viewed 1 July 2009, http://www.telegraph.co.uk/news/main.jhtml?xml=/news/2007/09/11/nstout111.xml.

McCrone, J 1994, 'Psychic powers: what are the odds?', *New Scientist*, 26 November, pp. 34–8.

McKie, R 2001, 'Royal Mail's Nobel guru in telepathy row', *Observer*, 30 September, viewed 1 July 2009, http://www.guardian.co.uk/uk/2001/sep/30/robinmckie.theobserver.

Miller, M, Pomerantz, D, and Rose, L 2009, *The celebrity 100*, Forbes, viewed 26 June 2009, http://www.forbes.com/2009/06/03/forbes-100-celebrity-09-jolie-oprah-madonna_land.html.

MPC (Minor Planets Center) 2009, *Minor planet names: alphabetical list*, Harvard–Smithsonian Center for Astrophysics, viewed 30 June 2009, http://www.cfa.harvard.edu/iau/lists/MPNames.html.

NLA (National Library of Australia) 2008, *Where can I find the most popular names in Australia?*, viewed 26 June 2009, http://www.nla.gov.au/infoserv/faq/index.php?sid=1526713&lang=en&action=artikel&cat=20&id=27102&artlang=en.

NSO (National Statistics Online) 2009, *Babies' names 2007*, NSO, viewed 26 June 2009, http://www.statistics.gov.uk/cci/nugget.asp?id=184.

Ogg, O 1963, *The 26 Letters*, E.M. Hale, Eau Claire, WI.

Pike, A and Cooper, R 1980, *Australian Film 1900–1977*, Oxford University Press, Melbourne.

Pinker, S 2008, *Paul Allen*, Time & CNN, viewed 1 July 2009, http://www.time.com/time/specials/2007/time100/article/0,28804,1595326_1595329_1616322,00.html.

PleaseSavePluto 2008, *Petition for immediate reversal of decision to demote Pluto...*, viewed 13 June 2008, http://pleasesavepluto.org/.

Roberts, C 2004, *Heavy Words Lightly Thrown: The reason behind the rhyme*, Granta Books, London.

Seligman, MEP, Parks, AC, and Steen, T 2005, 'A balanced psychology and a full life', in FA Huppert, N Baylis, and B Keverne (eds), *The Science of Well-being*, Oxford University Press. Oxford, pp. 274–83.

SSA (Social Security Administration) 2009, *Popular baby names 2008*, SSA, viewed 26 June 2009, http://www.ssa.gov/OACT/babynames/.

Steele, JM 2005, 'Darrell Huff and fifty years of *How to lie with statistics*', *Statistical Science*, vol. 20, no. 3, pp. 205–9.

Tankard, JW 1984, *The Statistical Pioneers*, Schenkman, Cambridge, MA.

The Economist, 2007, 'Where money seems to talk', 14 July, pp. 63–4.

THES-QS 2009, *World University Rankings: the methodology: a simple overview*, Quacquarelli Symonds, viewed 26 June 2009, http://www.topuniversities.com/worlduniversityrankings/methodology/simple_overview.

Tilley, R 1973, *A History of Playing Cards*, Studio Vista, London.

UN (United Nations) 2009a, *Growth in United Nations membership, 1945-present*, UN, viewed 24 June 2009, http://www.un.org/members/growth.shtml.

UN (United Nations) 2009b, *World population prospects: the 2008 revision population database*, viewed 25 June 2009, http://esa.un.org/unpp/index.asp?panel=1.

USCB (US Census Bureau) 2008a, *Annual estimates of the population for the United States, regions, states, and Puerto Rico: April 1, 2000 to July 1, 2008*, USCB, viewed 22 June 2009, http://www.census.gov/popest/states/NST-ann-est.html.

USCB (US Census Bureau) 2008b, *Income, poverty, and health insurance coverage in the United States: 2007*, USCB, viewed 1 July 2009, http://www.census.gov/prod/2008pubs/p60-235.pdf.

USMA (US Metric Association) 2009, *U.S. Metric Association*, viewed 1 July 2009, http://lamar.colostate.edu/~hillger/.

USPS (US Postal Service) 1998, *Official USPS abbreviations*, USPS, viewed 30 June 2009, http://www.usps.com/ncsc/lookups/usps_abbreviations.html.

Veenhoven, R 2000, 'What this journal is about', *Journal of Happiness Studies*, vol. 1, pp. v–viii.

Wells, MW nd, *Origins of the name 'Idaho' and how Idaho became a territory in 1863*, Idaho Museum of Natural History, viewed 22 June 2009, http://imnh.isu.edu/digitalatlas/geog/explore/essay.pdf.

WHO (World Health Organization) 2002, *Global solar UV index: a practical guide*, World Health Organization, Geneva, viewed 29 June 2009, http://www.unep.org/PDF/Solar_Index_Guide.pdf.

WHO (World Health Organization) 2008, *WHO report on the global tobacco epidemic, 2008*, World Health Organization, Geneva, viewed 1 July 2009, http://www.who.int/tobacco/mpower/mpower_report_full_2008.pdf.

Yates, F and Mather, K 1963, *Ronald Aylmer Fisher 1890–1962* (reprinted from *Biographical Memoirs of the Royal Society of London*, vol. 9, pp. 91–120), University of Adelaide, viewed 1 July 2009, www.adelaide.edu.au/library/special/digital/fisher/fisherbiog.pdf.

Zeisel, H 1985, *Say It With Figures* (6th edn), Harper & Row, New York.

Index